FROM BALLINROBE TO WEXFORD

An Englishman's travels around the Irish racecourses

By David Hawkins

Cover image and book design by Kate Hamilton

Printed in the United Kingdom

First Printing, 2024

ISBN: 978-1-7385165-0-6 (Paperback)
ISBN: 978-1-7385165-1-3 (eBook)

David Hawkins
Polegate, E. Sussex

Front cover image: The famous Bank course at Punchestown.

Back cover image: The village sign in County Tipperary confirming the Irish love of horse racing.

Ireland's Racecourses

Source: West, J. (2000). *Travelling the Turf: A Distinguished Companion to the Racecourses of Great Britain and Ireland.* Kensington West Productions Ltd, p 213, photograph © Bob Harrington.

The Author

David Hawkins has been an avid horse racing fan since the last year of the Arkle era in 1966. He has visited every racecourse in the UK and in the RoI, as well as many leading tracks in the EU, including Longchamp, Saint Cloud, Auteuil and Chantilly – all in France – and Pardubice in the Czech Republic. Having worked as a Chartered Accountant in East Sussex for over 40 years, he is now retired and free to roam racecourses and play plenty of golf. Furthermore, he has been able to focus on Irish racecourses – the subject of this book.

Disclaimer

Although every effort has been made to minimise the chances of any factual errors being reproduced in this book, neither the author nor any associated parties can accept legal – or any other – liability for any errors in the text that may have inadvertently arisen.

Acknowledgements

I am extremely grateful to my brother, Nigel, for so kindly editing my endless scripts and to his colleague, Kate Hamilton, for her tireless work in producing the book. I also want to thank my son, Matthew, and my daughter, Melanie, and my very dear friend, Debbie, for their inspiration and encouragement, which has enabled me finally to complete the book.

I would like to express my thanks to Sam Pearce at SWATT Books Ltd for her exceptional help with publishing this book. I am also appreciative of the help received from various racecourses.

December 2023

Contents

Introduction

As a young boy, my earliest memories of going to the races stretch back to a race meeting at Lingfield Park in May 1966 – it was the racecourse's highlight of the year, featuring the Derby Trial. I can recall the big race vividly, as the short-priced favourite, Charlottown, was given an uninspired ride by Ron Hutchinson – and narrowly beaten. Hutchinson returned to the unsaddling enclosure and received a decidedly unpleasant reception from various disgruntled punters. Some weeks later, fellow Australian, Scobie Breasley, was given the ride on Charlottown in the Derby at Epsom Downs. History records Charlottown as an impressive winner there.

By the time of the 1967 Grand National, I had caught the racing bug. The success of the totally unfancied Foinavon and the brilliant commentary on the BBC of Michael O'Hehir is still vivid in my memory, as he described the carnage at the 23rd fence with such amazing clarity. The blinkered and supposedly hopeless jumper, Foinavon, appeared out of the melee and managed to jump the remaining fences, albeit being a very lucky winner at odds of 100/1. But Foinavon did jump the 30 fences and last out the gruelling four and a half miles.

Having been brought up in East Sussex, Lingfield Park, Plumpton and Fontwell Park were regularly visited. Indeed, despite being sent to a boarding school just over the Kent border, Lingfield Park was very accessible during term-time. I used to go with my old school mate, Alastair Down, of Channel 4 and Racing Post fame.

In May 2008, he described his own memories of our trips in his amusing article in the Racing Post.

My mother used to pick us up at Saturday lunch-time; it was always a mad dash to get to the races, particularly in winter time due to the early starts. My mother was not known for her slow driving and used to get a fair turn of speed out of her Triumph Herald: Alastair reckoned the journey to the races was often as exciting as the racing itself. Both Alastair and I had a penchant for jump racing; we were at Lingfield Park in the early 1970s when The Dikler was establishing himself as a great chaser. There was the unforgettable memory of Stan Mellor desperately trying to steer the big horse around the sharp bend after the stands; he just managed to do so, losing considerable ground in the process. But The Dikler still won very easily.

Despite the confinements of boarding school, Alastair and I still managed to follow the racing closely. We were known to frequent the local Joe Coral betting shop. Finally, it became clear that a telephone account was the only way forward. However, it was hard work, as the morning paper tended to arrive shortly before we were due to attend chapel; there was only a 25-minute mid-morning break to make a necessary telephone call! And I was tempted, on occasions, to cut out the racing page from the paper and fold it up neatly, so that it could be read during a particularly boring sermon in chapel! Nonetheless, I never gambled very much and it was just a bit of fun to leave £10 with the bookmaker at the start of term. Occasionally, I was ahead at the end of term but was probably still out of pocket as I had fed many 2p coins into the telephone during the term!

Since leaving school, I have only bet in small amounts. After all, there are few poor bookmakers around – something my father continually stated. In fact, his viewpoint was re-affirmed last year by the news that Denise Coates, the chief executive of BET365, was paid a salary of £213 million in 2022, as well as receiving dividends amounting to a mere £45 million! Mind you, it is the second successive year that she has taken a pay-cut, since she earned £421 million in 2020 which fell to a more modest £250 million in 2021!

In my view, the average punter is ill-informed about very relevant aspects of the horses about to run, particularly regarding their fitness. There are many horses running, with virtually no chance of winning; this is especially true in Ireland.

Despite living very near the English Channel for all my life, I have had the opportunity to travel up-and-down the country. As such, I have been able to visit all the racecourses in England, Scotland and Wales. By 1996, I had completed the full-set of visits to the 60 racecourses, including both of Newmarket's racecourses. To complete the list, I went to Ayr in style, by driving with my mother to Stansted and flying to Prestwick. My mother had never been to Scotland and I do not think she was inclined revisit it, after being thrust a grubby copy of the Daily Mirror by the taxi-driver at the airport. His paper was opened at the racing page and he asked her, in a thick Glaswegian accent that she could barely understand, to mark the 'effing' card. The day was particularly memorable for a superb exhibition of jumping from the stunning-looking grey, The Grey Monk, with Tony Dobbin perched on top as he flew over the fences; he won easily, with his rivals stretched way down the track. What a shame that the horse never fulfilled his potential by winning a really big race.

More recently, two new courses have emerged – Chelmsford (formerly Great Leighs) and Ffos Las, to the north west of Swansea: both of these I have now visited. The variety of the racecourses in this country is what makes them interesting: exactly the same applies in Ireland. Whilst I have never visited the US, the thought of attending meetings where every track seems to be left-handed, flat and about one mile round bores me; moreover, many races there are run on dirt, another turn-off. Indeed, I am regularly searching for the 'off' button on my TV control, whenever 'Stateside' starts on Sky TV!

I would mention, though, that there are a few courses here which do not inspire me. I went to Epsom Downs in the mid-1970s and vowed never to return. It was Oaks day, which – at that time – was held two days after the Derby. The racecourse was covered in litter blowing around, as well as being populated by various dodgy-looking characters trying to sell jewellery or other junk; it was somewhat reminiscent of a third-rate boot-fair. In fact, I did return a few years ago and appreciated some much-needed improvements – Epsom Downs has gone up in my estimation! In truth, several Midlands and Northern racecourses are drab and lacklustre. Nottingham, for example, abandoned jump racing some years ago, and now subsists on a diet of low-grade Flat meetings; Wolverhampton now hosts poor-quality, all-weather racing; along with Southwell, which occasionally stages jump meetings on turf; and Leicester hosts racing all-year round, with the very occasional quality race. Further north, Redcar uses its straight course for most races, in common with Newmarket, so you see little racing at close range.

Further south, 'lovely Lingfield', as it was once known, lost many of its trees in the great storm of 1987. Subsequently, it decided both to eliminate most of the remainder and to carve out a sand track in the centre of the racecourse, which stages many all-weather meetings – with the main aim presumably of keeping the betting shops busy. Sadly, Kempton Park has gone down a similar route – the quality of its racing has deteriorated sharply. Thankfully, though, its major Christmas meeting endures. Importantly, some interesting and quirky tracks in

Britain survive, both on the Flat and over the jumps. Within this category, are Bath, Brighton and Chester on the Flat with track lay-outs, which are certainly challenging for jockeys. Regrettably, I never managed to visit Alexandra Palace in the north of London before its demise in 1970, but the famous and very tight 'frying pan' track at 'Ally Pally' must have been quite a sight, even if it was notoriously dangerous.

There are various jumping racecourses in Britain, with their own idiosyncrasies. They include Fontwell Park and its figure of eight lay-out, on the chase course; the tough two-mile circuit at Exeter; the tiny tracks at Cartmel and Fakenham; the sweeping acres of Newbury, Sandown Park, Haydock Park and Doncaster; the undulating ground at Chepstow and Cheltenham; and, of course, the toughest test of all at Aintree, the home of the Grand National. Many of the smaller jump racecourses have real character, such as Kelso, Perth, Hexham, Stratford, Ludlow, Bangor-on-Dee and Plumpton: all have a good local following. Overall, racing fans should be very grateful for what British courses offer. We can only hope that the current economic downturn and the legacy of COVID-19 do not result in any of them closing or adopting the bookmaker-orientated – and depressing – all-weather conversion scenario.

Not surprisingly, Ireland's racecourses are similar in the variety that they offer. There are 27 courses, although it is very difficult to locate Laytown's 'racecourse' – or even to call it as such – as it consists of a one-day annual fixture that is run on the beach. Furthermore, Tralee has apparently been closed down for good, even though there is a remote possibility that it will be re-established, since the proposed building development promised over a decade ago has still not started.

In 1991, I first went horse racing in Ireland. By November 2008, I had completed the tour of all its racecourses – and quite a tour it proved to be. Hence, the reason for an attempt to relate my story, which has taken a long time to come to fruition! Part of the title of my book replicates Stephen Cartmell's excellent book, 'From Aintree to York', in which he recounts his travels to all of Britain's racecourses.

Unlike in the US, for example, horse racing in Britain and in Ireland is very similar, but there are a few distinguishing features that merit comment:

1. It is seldom in Ireland that more than one meeting takes place daily, although there is a recent trend for more days with two meetings, particularly at week-ends or on Bank Holidays;
2. From November through to February in Ireland, there are just one or two meetings during the week; most meetings are staged at week-ends. This profile has changed in recent years, with the unfortunate proliferation of

meetings on the all-weather surface at Dundalk during the winter;

3. In the summer, many meetings in Ireland are evening events. In the past, there were numerous mixed meetings – including both jumping and Flat racing – but these have been reduced in number, partly to save the costs of hiring starting-stalls for just one race or two;

4. Virtually all jump meetings in Ireland consist of seven races, with the last race being a bumper, which is a Flat race, normally over two miles, and with the horses being amateur-ridden;

5. The going is described slightly differently in Ireland, in that one common description is 'yielding to soft', which is broadly equivalent to 'heavy' in Britain. The Irish concept of 'heavy' is often more accurately described as water-logged over here and may lead to an abandonment;

6. The racecourse lay-out varies little between Britain and Ireland. While there are no water jumps on Irish jump tracks, there are open-ditch obstacles; these are known as regulation fences;

7. Irish racecourses use a weigh-room, rather than a weighing room as in Britain. The 'white flag is raised' when they are under 'starter's order', and the normal announcement after a race is 'winner alright' rather than the usual 'weighed-in' used on the British side of the Irish Sea;

8. Entry prices to Irish racecourses are slightly lower than those in Britain, once allowance is made for the €/£ exchange rate. Typically, course entrance fees might be €15 in Ireland compared with around £20 in Britain. Car parks in Ireland are generally free: given the dreadful state of some of them, this seems fair. In Britain, more racecourses charge for car parking;

9. Another unique feature of Irish racecourses is that there will often be a group of ladies trying to sell you chocolate and fruit, as you leave the racecourse after the end of racing. You may also find ladies in the car parks attempting to sell over-priced race cards, on the spurious basis that it has a good tip inside – but this seems to be typical Irish blarney!

The quality of racing in Ireland is often higher than that in Britain. Races in the former are generally more competitive, with larger fields, even on tight tracks where significantly different rules regarding safety limits seem to apply. Rarely does a meeting in Ireland consist of many races with less than 10 runners per race. There is a view, too, that more meetings could be scheduled, since many races have suffered from horses being balloted out of them; this scenario seems to be changing, following the negative impact of both COVID-19 and the recent economic recession.

Normally, the only occasions in Ireland when races are short of runners occur when the ground dries out and the going becomes 'firm' – not exactly a regular occurrence in Ireland, which attracts more than its fair share of wet weather! Indeed, I understand that watering of many Irish racecourses is not standard. I can only assume that tackling water-logging is such a priority that little thought is given to preventing firm ground.

Interestingly, there are several Irish racecourses, which – despite staging jump racing – do not race at all throughout the winter; this is primarily to enable the track to be rested during the really wet winter months; otherwise, they would become the proverbial 'Irish Bog'. Only The Curragh, Dundalk and Laytown do not stage jump racing so that leaves 24 courses (23 excluding Tralee), of which around half hold meetings between the end of October and the following March.

The fixture list seems carefully tailored to attract good crowds. Hence, it is not worthwhile to stage a meeting on a Monday in January, for example. By contrast, in Britain, you should expect at least one meeting on an all-weather track to be held daily – where the number of spectators is almost exceeded by the number of runners. The pre-ponderance of evening meetings in Ireland also means events are generally well-attended. By way of example, Dundalk has recently started holding regular Friday evening meetings under lights: its fixture list has increased considerably.

In my view, only one or two courses in Ireland can be described as dreary – unlike on this side of the Irish Sea, where are several. All 27 of the Irish racecourses are worth a visit – I shall describe my own tour of them. Most offer good-class racing, an interesting and variable card, along with a warm welcome – but with few frills other than at the likes of Leopardstown, The Curragh, Fairyhouse, Punchestown and Galway. The emphasis remains on the quality of the horse racing rather than on the facilities. Generally, there is no need to dress up (only at the top courses is there a dress code for special enclosures) but an effort should be made to wear practical and warm clothing.

Travelling to Ireland to watch the horse racing can be quite entertaining: the easiest method is generally booking via Ryanair or another similar low-cost carrier. Ticket prices used to be remarkably low. I have often travelled to Dublin and back from Gatwick Airport, paying less than the cost of a return rail fare between the East Sussex coast and London. The rail journey is barely 60 miles each way and takes longer than the flight – and is regularly crowded making it difficult to find a seat! In recent years, though still very cheap, prices have risen sharply. With higher costs, including Air Passenger Duty, the £1.99 which I once paid for a return flight is highly improbable to recur.

The airports at Dublin and Shannon are the two best airports to choose; however, it does involve a minor trek to reach the likes of Roscommon and Sligo. With the M4 and then the M6 extending across the centre of Ireland, Roscommon is now much easier to access. Surprisingly, it takes barely two hours to reach either of the two racecourses – Down Royal and Downpatrick – in Northern Ireland (NI). Although several courses highlight local train stations, I have only travelled once on a train in Ireland – my sole journey was a non-racing day-trip to Belfast from Drogheda. The train network in Ireland did not develop at either the speed or extent of its growth in Britain; connections, therefore, are much trickier outside the main towns. Hiring a car has, therefore, been my preferred option.

Hiring a car in Ireland should be simple but a word of warning – do check out the car that you are given carefully! If you collect a car in mid-morning and happily drive off to the nearby racecourse, I can tell you – from experience – that it is more than disconcerting when you leave in the gathering gloom that the headlights are faulty! I faced this challenge one November day when I was driving back from Punchestown to Dublin, as it was getting dark. Fortunately, it was only 30 miles or so back to Dublin, but the downside was that the only way I could drive was on undipped lights. Not surprisingly, I was regularly flashed by oncoming vehicles. On returning the car, I explained my problem to the hire-car employee at the airport. He seemed somewhat surprised at my anxiety that it was a serious problem but was more than happy – without any undue persuasion – to refund my hire-car cost: I was left to pay solely for the petrol used!

On another occasion, I was about to drive off when I realised that the left-hand wing mirror was hanging off and banging against the bottom of the side door. When I mentioned this issue, a mechanic came out in a flash, brandishing a screw-driver; he fixed the offending item in no time at all! Almost without exception, I have found Irish people delightfully kind and helpful but they can be so laid-back! Nothing ever seems much of a problem to them!

If you have never driven in the Republic of Ireland (RoI), you should be aware that road signs are few. Rarely is there more than one and, if you miss a turning, you may not be given a second chance. Often, the signs are installed in awkward places, being buried, for example, in hedges and trees.

To be fair, roads in the RoI have improved significantly in recent years: my early visits to the RoI involved considerable driving along very bumpy roads. Previously, repairing potholes generally consisted of tipping a small pile of tarmac into the offending hole; often, this left either a protruding mound or a large crater, both of which were difficult to avoid, especially in the dark. Over the last 15 years or so, there has been a major road building programme, which has led to many towns being by-passed. Several motorways, including the M50 around Dublin – which seeks to emulate London's M25 – have been built. Much of this infrastructure has been funded by the EU. Like London's M25, the M50 seemed always to be unfinished but, following my last visit in 2022, I believe it is now finished. My latest trip to Ireland took place in November 2022, when, in five days or so, I called in at 24 of the 27 racecourses there. I attended three race meetings and I only missed out visiting Galway, Ballinrobe and Sligo. Undoubtedly, the road improvements over the last decade or so made this trip far easier.

If you do have time on the way to a racecourse, you are bound to pass many pubs in which you are almost sure to be welcomed – and no doubt be given plenty of tips if you let on that you are going to the races! But paying for lunch in a pub may need patience. While staff are generally quick enough to take an order for sandwiches or more substantial meals, payment is often deferred until you have finished. And it can be quite a wait to find someone willing to take your money; they sometimes say 'oh, do you want to pay?' When you do, you are thanked profusely. Be careful, too, if you stop at a village shop to buy a newspaper, because the owner may want a chat: if you are third in the queue, then you may have ten minutes or so to wait.

Despite their various trials and tribulations, I can assure you that race meetings in Ireland are certainly worth attending. There is the whole package on show – generally good-quality and competitive horse racing on mainly attractive courses in a relaxed atmosphere. I cannot recall having attended an Irish race meeting and regretted it, even when I had backed every conceivable loser on the card! Some years ago, this view point was endorsed by an acquaintance, who attended all five days of the Listowel Festival meeting (it is now seven days' duration). He failed to back a single winner but avowed that it was the most enjoyable horse racing he had ever attended. Furthermore, he was a serious race-goer and always sought to beat the bookmakers: on this occasion at Listowel, he palpably failed to do so. Overall, in my experience, the Irish people are fun-loving by nature and even their indifferent weather rarely dampens their spirits – their enthusiasm is unlimited. In short, to use Irish terminology, they expect the whole day to be good craic. If you have not been racing in Ireland, could I suggest you make plans to do so – I will be very surprised if you return disappointed!

1

Ballinrobe

Sweeping into Ballinrobe's home straight.

The racecourse at Ballinrobe, unlike some in Ireland, is extremely easy to find as you take the N84 out of the town and head north on the Castlebar road – the course is about one mile away on the left-hand side. Just north of the course, the N84 goes between Lough Mask and Lough Carra and there is a turn to the left to Westport. Just south of Ballinrobe, you will find the stunning Lough Corrib which stretches down almost to Galway itself. A little further west and you are soon in the sparsely populated Connemara National Park and the peaks of the Twelve Bens mountains.

On the west side of Lough Mask sits the small town of Toormakeady from where an old business contact of mine, Willy Gibbons, hails. He assures me that you must climb the peak of Croag Patrick, south-west of Westport. It is over 2,000 feet high and he tells me you can see 360 islands if you care to count them all – I regret I have not yet had a chance to find out whether my leg is being pulled or not! It is clearly a dramatic but peaceful setting and is quite similar to the Lake District in England. The Ballinrobe course itself reminds me of Cartmel, not least for the prevalence of the attractive dry stone walls which are highly visible around both courses.

There is a long history of racing in Ballinrobe, with a record of a meeting as far back as 1774 although the present course was not used until 1921. For many years, it was very much a country track, ignored by the big stables, but it was clearly highly popular with the local fraternity. In the late 1960s, it appears there was even the prospect of closure. However, the locals fought hard against such a plan and it is good to see they have been handsomely rewarded. There was a significant – and much-needed – upgrade in 1998 which transformed the drab and basic facilities to something much more comfortable and attractive – that is where the similarity to Cartmel probably ends with no major investment being undertaken at the Cumbrian track for some time, apart from a rebuilt grandstand in 2004.

Ballinrobe now has all the facilities of a well-organised track with a good size paddock, a large stand, plenty of bars and ample parking. One particular feature is that there still seems to be a lot of space, even though large crowds are regularly attracted to each meeting. Yet, despite the major investment, the course has kept its charm and has not changed its identity of being a country racecourse. Furthermore, it seems very pro-active in obtaining sponsorship from the local business community. The course is clearly on the up and further funding from Horse Racing Ireland has meant additional facilities and upgrades; in short, it seems very well-placed going forward. Annual membership for 2023 was priced at €110 for 10 meetings and 18 reciprocal meetings elsewhere in Ireland and Britain, plus a race card: this seems very reasonable, to say the least.

The track itself used to be a simple oval of about nine furlongs round. It was easily visible from both the stands and at ground level. The ground rises as the runners move out of the back straight, before dropping downhill as they round the bend into the short finishing straight. However, in recent years, an outer loop has been constructed on the back straight mainly for the steeplechase track with the inner loop being used for Flat and hurdle races. The steeplechase track provides a good spectacle with two fences to jump as they round the bend and straighten up for the short downhill run to the winning post, which is located half-way along the straight in front of the stands. This finish is also quite different from Cartmel which is famous for its half-mile run-in! Overall, the course is generally very good for viewing, primarily due to its size, but there is the added attraction of the spectacular backdrop of the famous Partry Mountains and surrounding countryside. The only downside may be that the new loop on the steeplechase course is on the far side of some very large trees. The stands are more than adequate and, in fact, there is a good view of the racing from ground level, with the runners never appearing to be very far away.

I was at Ballinrobe for the first day of the July meeting in 2002, which had a seven-race card starting at 6pm on a pleasantly warm evening. The card comprised good variety with four Flat races followed by a novice chase, a maiden hurdle and the inevitable bumper for the finale. There were the usual competitive fields with 15 or 16 runners in every race and a large crowd for a Monday evening so there was a great atmosphere. You would find it very difficult to find such enthusiasm at a racecourse on this side of the Irish Sea on a Monday evening – Windsor might be an exception.

The crowd was easily absorbed and even though it was five or six deep around the paddock, I was still surprised that a small man in the paddock should recognise me. The gentleman concerned was Michael Hourigan, who was training a horse for one of my relatives in which I had a minor interest. He motioned to me to meet when he had left the paddock and with his usual bonhomie brought me up to date on our horse's condition. It also transpired that he was a good supporter of Ballinrobe races and had brought four runners up from his stables near Limerick. Indeed, one of his former stable stars, Doran's Pride, had her first-ever win at Ballinrobe in 1993.

More recently, I was at Ballinrobe for the evening meeting on the first day of May 2012. The weather was rather drab, with light rain showers, but this did not stop a healthy crowd from attending and it was noticeable that further improvements had been made since my last visit. There is an impressive new weigh-room along with the Coranna Restaurant offering corporate hospitality facilities. The building is very attractively designed with a tower on top and a large old-fashioned clock although – unfortunately – it had stopped!

The drab evening was lit up by one of the geniuses of Irish racing in the shape of Paul Carberry, who rode the winner in four of the first six races. It was vintage riding and typically three of the winners only took the lead in the shadow of the winning post, whereas his other winner won so easily that even he could not stop his rather lovely named mount, Turnonthegas, from winning by over seven lengths despite sitting motionless in the saddle.

Carberry may have been controversial and not as consistent as the likes of Ruby Walsh and Tony McCoy. On his day, though, he seemed to possess an ability above that of his more illustrious colleagues. His first winner, Six Stone Ned, in the maiden hurdle was tenderly ridden in the middle of the field and produced just at the right time to win by about two lengths. His second, Fairymount Lord, was ridden the same way but made a mistake at the last and just got up to win by a head. On returning to the winner's enclosure, there were various comments of 'well ridden' to Carberry, who was then heard to remark 'I nearly buggered that one up didn't I?'

Having won easily on Turnonthegas, his most sensational ride was on Croskeagh Royale in the 14-runner beginners' chase. The horse had not run for nearly 18 months and was given a sympathetic ride but was only seventh as they left the back straight for the final two fences and he still had four horses ahead of him at the last. Somehow, he appeared from nowhere on the shortish downhill run-in and got up near the post to win by a neck – a truly amazing ride!

You can only be impressed by a visit to Ballinrobe – there is little to say against it other than that the standard of racing could be higher but it seems to be improving as the course's reputation continues to be enhanced. It should also be mentioned that Tiger Roll, the two-time Grand National winner, won his first race over fences at the track in 2016. What really makes it a great course is its idyllic setting – there are not many more lovely places to be on a sunny summer's evening than at Ballinrobe races with the sun gently fading in the west over the Partry Mountains opposite the stands and the horses gleaming in their bright summer coats!

Each year, the racing season starts in April and lasts until September; therefore, there is no racing in the winter when rain could well be pouring across the course with the help of a westerly gale! In 2023, there were 10 meetings scheduled and they were all on week-day afternoons or evenings – clearly the management can see this is the best way to attract a good crowd! The old policy of holding mixed meetings seems to have been largely phased out, so that some days are purely Flat meetings and the others purely for jumping: the feature race of the season is the Mayo National Chase worth about €50,000. The course seems to be becoming ever popular and certainly Willy Gibbons and his family, who live in Sussex, make a point of going home and timing their visit to fit in with Ballinrobe races and enjoying the good craic! So, the message is travel there and I will be amazed if you are disappointed – the weather could be the only reason!

While you are in this beautiful part of Ireland and, if like me, you fancy some golf, I can recommend that you combine a visit to the races with a round at Ballinrobe Golf Club, which is some two or three miles east of the racecourse. It is set in a 300-acre estate, known as Cloonacastle, with the River Robe running alongside the golf course. There are several interesting holes as well as large estate buildings, including the clubhouse and the inevitable large bar, which is undoubtedly an important part of all Irish golf courses as well as their racecourses. In the past, the Ballinrobe racecourse executive had offered a package with the golf club whereby a round of golf, racecourse admission – together with a two-course meal and a race card – was priced at €45 on the 2012 racecourse website. It may still be available but no doubt at a somewhat higher price!

2

Bellewstown

Bleak stands – the legendary phone box at Bellewstown is on the far left.

First of all, let's get the pronunciation right – it is BELL-ewstown – and it is situated some 25 miles north of Dublin and about six miles south-west of the busy town of Drogheda. The racecourse, though, is pretty much in the middle of nowhere sitting high up on a hill known as the Hill of Crockafotha and is apparently some 700 feet above sea level – strangely enough, it is quite similar to where my father was brought up in Knockholt, Kent, which is also high up but is only 20 miles or so from Central London; it is hard to believe you are so close to a big city.

It has been said that, from the racecourse, you can see out to the Irish Sea and as far north as the Mountains of Mourne but I had not noticed this view and certainly not in the excitement of a crowded evening race meeting. However, on my last visit in November 2022, I drove north past the back of the stands and there, indeed, is the most stunning view of the coastline stretching north and – in the distance – are the Mountains of Mourne in NI. I also rather like the message on the back of the stands which states there has been horse racing on the 'Hill' since 1726!

Despite its remote location, it is reasonably easy to access the racecourse providing you can navigate along the various lanes which converge at the top of the hill. In fact, there seem to be about five roads, up steep gradients from various directions, which congregate around the racecourse. Let's be honest, you will not get lost trying to find the course when racing is on because the meetings are all hugely popular.

From Dublin, it is merely a case of following the vastly improved road north, which is now the M1, and then exiting at the signs for Drogheda South and Julianstown. You then join the old N1 before signs appear for Bellewstown – if in doubt, you only have to look for the steep hill! Follow the crowd seems to be the mantra, as finding the racecourse when there is no racing is nothing like as simple! My favourite access is from the north and turning off the R150 road from Duleek to Julianstown. You go over a very attractive stone bridge crossing a stream and then head steadily uphill for a mile or two past various large properties with pretty rhododendron hedges and well-matured trees. Suddenly, the view ahead opens out and you find yourself crossing the back straight of the racecourse. When there is no racing, which is almost 360 days of the year, you can park in the middle of the course and will soon discover it is popular with walkers and particularly with dog-owners!

For many years, the course held just an annual three-day fixture in early July but, 10 years or so ago, a two-day meeting in August was instituted. More recently, further racing days have been added with the 2023 fixture list showing a meeting in April and two days at the end of September – which is good to see – as well as the July and August fixtures: the latter are likely to be well-patronised and there is also a tendency for the meetings to be held in the evening.

The course at Bellewstown is unusual in Ireland in that it has just Flat and hurdle races with the steeplechase course being scrapped some years ago due to the scarcity of meetings and the cost of maintaining the fences. Each day's card, therefore, tended to have a mixture of racing with some hurdle races and the remainder being on the Flat. In recent times, the course's management has tried to put on either hurdle or Flat racing on each day as the Irish Racing authorities are trying to cut down on the number of mixed racing days to save costs on items, such as the use of stalls and their handlers.

To be sure, the facilities at the racecourse are fairly basic which is not surprising considering its limited use. There are two stands, which really do look past their 'sell-by' dates; they remind me of the stands when I went to the football at Middlesbrough's old ground at Ayresome Park which was demolished nearly 30 years ago. I imagine the stands at Bellewstown are of a similar vintage and can best be described as functional and particularly unattractive: but with meetings in July and August, they should not normally be required to shelter race-goers from bad weather. Otherwise, there are marquees erected for the race days and particularly for the hospitality trade; they seem extremely popular since the course, being quite close to Dublin, attracts many race-goers. Plenty of use is also made of the Bellewstown Inn on the other side of the country lane which runs down the home straight. Sadly, though, on my visit to the course in November 2008, it looked like it could well have witnessed its last racing day as it had been destroyed by fire. I was relieved to see it was clearly back in business when I was last there.

Similarly, like Ballinrobe, the course has quite a connection with Cartmel in that there is plenty of entertainment put on for the children with a fun-fair and other attractions for the July meeting in particular. Whilst I am not a great fan of this idea, I will admit it enables the whole family to go racing and Dad can attend to the challenging matter of trying to back winners as well – no doubt – as consuming a few pints of Guinness while Mum looks after the children. At least, the fun-fair is tucked away at the side of the course towards the one-furlong pole and does not intrude, to any great extent, on the more serious side of the racing itself. There is generally a large crowd because of the time of the year and there is not a lot of free space but it seems to be cleverly used and you do not feel unduly enclosed. But there are high railings around the whole of the main enclosure and stands, which – for some – can be off-putting.

The course itself is left-handed and about nine furlongs round, with five hurdles per circuit. There is a chute for the five-furlong Flat track, which joins the main circuit about three furlongs from home near the entrance to the home straight. I should add that it is not exactly a straight five-furlong course as most of it lies on a gentle curve. In fact, there are hardly any straight five or six-furlong Flat courses in Ireland, unlike in England. The round course at Bellewstown is generally flat but some of the bends are quite sharp, particularly after the winning post and my amateurish mind suggests that they could be rather treacherous on hard or slippery ground.

My main gripe about the racecourse is that it is not the easiest for viewing despite being a relatively small track. The field effectively disappears from sight when the horses are half-way down the back straight and only reappear some three furlongs later as they turn into the straight - unless you are right up in the rafters of one of the old stands. The problem has generally been that the centre of the course is covered in gorse, shrubs and trees which could do with the attention of a decent tree surgeon to trim them down to a reasonable level. To be fair, it does seem, based on my more recent visits, that some attempt has been made to deal with this issue. I appreciate that, in the 21st century, most courses tend to use a giant screen showing the racing but it does seem a shame that you cannot enjoy a better view of the racing merely because the height of the trees and gorse is out of control.

Bellewstown has a long history of racing; there is evidence of activity going as far back as 1726. Bizarrely, its most famous item is the old telephone box which stands proudly to the right of the stands. This scenario is all based on the amazing betting coup landed by that great character, Barney Curley, in 1975 with a horse by the name of Yellow Sam: it has come to prominence again recently, following Curley's death. Yellow Sam was handled by an obscure trainer, Liam Brennan, and was aimed at an amateur riders' race at Bellewstown: with little form, it was priced at 20/1. Curley organised a gang of men to go round betting shops all over Ireland and to place large amounts of money on Yellow Sam, whose starting price would be based on the average price offered by the bookies actually on the course. Before the days of mobile phones, Bellewstown had only one public phone box and, apparently, no other landline connections. Curley arranged for one of his friends to occupy the phone box up to the starting-time of the race to ensure that there was no chance of the off-course bookies contacting their on-course colleagues, thereby reducing Yellow Sam's starting price. This telephone box was therefore a crucial part of the coup.

The horse, of course, still had to win – and win it did reasonably comfortably, with Curley watching the race from about two furlongs down the course hidden amongst the gorse bushes. The jockey, Michael Furlong, was quite oblivious to the coup but, after the race, he was quickly picked up by Curley's entourage and driven away before anything was said or questions were asked. Curley reputedly won over 325,000 Irish Punts which – in today's money – would equate to over £3 million. This coup set him up for buying a large property in Ireland and then, in time, moving over to the UK and living in Newmarket where he trained horses.

The only meeting that I have attended at Bellewstown was with my son on the first day of the July Festival in 2000. I had not appreciated that this date was the 25th anniversary of Curley's coup over the bookmakers. However, the management remembered the date and referred to it in the race-card – and seemed to take pleasure in saying 'it was hard to believe that it's all of 25 years since Yellow Sam won on the Hill'. The quality of runners was not exactly high but there was an interesting and competitive card consisting of two hurdle races, four Flat races and the inevitable bumper being divided into two races; hence, eight races in all. The first race was at 5.30pm and the finale at 9pm. As expected, there was a substantial crowd on a warm and, more importantly, dry evening but there was just about enough space to see the action. The highlight was a driving finish to the handicap hurdle which, according to the betting, was a two-horse race. However, a young and inexperienced Ruby Walsh showed his brilliance on a 12/1 shot to squeeze past the two favourites and to shade it in a photo-finish according to the judge – much to the excitement of my son who had invested some of his pocket money on the winner. It was certainly a lovely way to spend a summer's evening!

In truth, Bellewstown really is worth a visit with its spectacular setting and quirky course even if the quality of the racing is not up to the standard of many other Irish racecourses: I certainly enjoyed my visit there. It is very much a course for holiday-makers attending the July and August meetings with plenty of other activities underway; it is very reminiscent of the holiday meetings which take place at Cartmel. There are, though, corporate hospitality facilities along with marquees for well-dressed guests. After all, the course is only a short drive from Dublin and from NI, with the M1 now fully operational. Whether this trend will continue is debatable, given the tighter regulations on corporate entertaining. The racecourse itself seems to be thriving and the recent expansion from three days to eight days racing per year is very encouraging – but the stands really could be demolished and something more attractive and functional should be erected in their place. Bellewstown has also benefitted from the Barney Curley legacy since, in the last year, two special races have been run. Furthermore, Frankie Dettori, who treated Curley as a father – figure from their time in Newmarket, made a special appearance at the course. This naturally meant an extra-large crowd, and Dettori capped it by riding a winner and then celebrating – inevitably – with his trade-mark flying dismount!

While you are in Bellewstown and for the golfers amongst you, there is a pitch-and-putt course amongst the gorse in the middle of the racecourse. When I first went to Bellewstown, the holes were only about 60 yards long (they are measured in the dreaded metres) and it looked easy to lose plenty of balls! The greens were about half the size of my lounge floor and surrounded by thick gorse bushes – I did not fancy my chances but it is not much easier picking winners on the racecourse either! In recent years, it seems that common sense has prevailed. Much of the gorse has been cleared away and the course looks eminently playable without needing too large a stock of balls – indeed, it looks quite fun!

3

Clonmel

Clonmel's paddock against a rural backdrop.

I first visited Clonmel in the early 1990s before the by-pass around the town was opened; it was clearly an area largely dependent on agriculture as every other vehicle in the town seemed to be either one covered in mud or a tractor. Indeed, there were plenty of tractors parked in the town with their owners presumably attending to the necessities of life, such as buying a newspaper (probably the Racing Post) or calling in at a favourite watering-hole for a pint of Guinness.

More recently, Clonmel has become of national interest this side of the Irish Sea as it has been prominently portrayed as the home of Magners cider. There was the splendid advert stressing the importance of transporting the apples to the cider press as quickly as possible, to the extent that the lorry driver buries a golfer's ball into the ground as he veers across a golf course, then skirts around a road via the fields before proceeding to drive through the wall at the entrance to the factory rather than through the open gate alongside – bizarre is the only word which springs to mind! Other even stranger adverts kept on appearing but let's be honest, the net result is a lovely pint of cider.

Clonmel racecourse is one of three in the County of Tipperary, along with Thurles and Tipperary itself. I notice from some maps that County Tipperary is divided into North and South and that Clonmel is only just in South Tipperary, by the border with County Waterford. It is located roughly half-way between Waterford and Limerick, sitting on the attractive River Suir which flows out to sea at Waterford. The area is spectacular with the town nestling in a valley below the Comeragh Mountains to the south, which are visible from the racecourse. North-east of the racecourse is the mountain of Slievenamon, standing at well over 2,000 feet; it is not so easy to see from the course, which is surprisingly straightforward to find. It is sited on the N24 town by-pass and, if you are coming from the east, you pass the vast Magners/Bulmers cider plant which looks like an industrial estate on its own – and there is a beautiful aroma, which hangs, as you drive past; it is especially for cider lovers!

If you arrive from the west, perhaps from Limerick or Tipperary, then you will come to a round-about on the N24 town by-pass; this is marked by a lovely piece of artwork in its centre showing a hurdle and a winning post. You can also turn off at the round-about to one of the biggest Tesco outlets that I have ever seen – the car park is vast and the store itself is about the size of a football pitch. I went there on my last visit in November 2022; it was a week-day at around 10am and there were only 15 cars parked in torrential rain, along with a Force 10 gale. Inside, it was hard to see any customers or staff but I was reminded that you cannot buy alcohol in Irish supermarkets before 10.30am so maybe that was partly the reason for the minimal foot-fall although the appalling weather was clearly the main issue.

I used to enjoy a good view of the famous Slievenamon from the house where my relatives lived for several years – some 10 miles up the road at the splendidly named Mullinahone. Their farmhouse was just off one of the bog roads out of Mullinahone which – inevitably – was not exactly well sign-posted when I first tried to find it on a wet Saturday night in the dark on my way back from the races at The Curragh. In desperation, I called in at one of the village pubs and picked up the telephone which did have some wires; unfortunately, they were not connected to anything of use. Hence, I asked for directions at the bar where a handful of locals were enjoying their pint. One of them asked me whether I was a Catholic priest to which I answered in the negative but I did add that I had seen plenty of them earlier in the day at The Curragh! Having said that, the locals kindly gave me some directions which must have been adequate since I somehow stumbled upon the farmhouse and a much-needed bed for the night!

I apologise for the digression but it does give an insight into the real Ireland, its countryside and the rustic folk of Tipperary. Clonmel racecourse certainly lives up to that image with traditionally Irish racing ground, by which I mean a veritable 'bog' that seems to be generously described as 'yielding to soft' or occasionally 'soft to heavy' and even occasionally 'heavy'. The Irish 'heavy' can probably be compared more accurately with the English 'water-logged' although it does seem that, these days, the Irish racing authorities are more prepared to cancel meetings, whereas 10 or 20 years ago they raced on ground more reminiscent of the battlefields on The Somme during the First World War.

The Clonmel course itself has a long history going back some 150 years and, for many years, was called Powerstown Park; it only changed its name to Clonmel in the late 1970s/early 1980s. I am not sure about the necessity to change racecourse names but at least a lot more people would know Clonmel rather than Powerstown Park! The venue is typical parkland, as its former name suggests, and it sits in a very attractive setting with plenty of large trees; there is a long row of tall fir trees on the outside of the track after the runners turn away from the finishing straight. Overall, the whole setting is heavily wooded. The track is right-handed and about one and a quarter miles round, with a steep rise past the fir trees before the runners reach the back straight.

I recall, in particular, the superb view of the runners in the back straight, as they appear to be on the skyline before descending the hill and then rounding the bend into the home straight and its steady uphill finish. The view from the paddock in the other direction is also stunning as you see a steep hillside on the other side of the River Suir, with animals grazing and farm buildings dotted around giving a general feeling of peace and tranquillity.

I first attended Clonmel races, as I note from the race card, in December 1997. I remember that the ground was very soft and muddy. Several horses slipped up or were brought down in a melee on the bend just after the stands in the opening race, which was a maiden hurdle – but thankfully there were no serious injuries either to horses or to riders. One of the leading riders in England at the time, Richard Dunwoody, travelled over from England for three rides and must have regretted it as all his mounts ran badly and never looked like winning. As usual, it was an interesting card and there was good competitive racing despite the desperate ground; not surprisingly, it was difficult to back winners. But there was a decent crowd for a mid-week meeting considering the poor weather – the executive at Wolverhampton for example, an all-weather course, would have been ecstatic if they had attracted such a crowd!

The facilities appeared quite basic and tired but the paddock looked particularly attractive even in early December. There was major investment soon after my initial visit as a new grandstand, bar and catering facilities were constructed: the weigh-room and turn-stile were also modernised. This investment took place in 1998 and I could certainly see its benefits on my last visit there in March 2017.

The course had 12 days of racing scheduled for 2023 and they were predominantly in the winter months as there were only two meetings between early April and the beginning of September. The meetings are mainly jumping, with just the occasional days of Flat racing. Top stables support the track and there are some important races in the jumping calendar with the highlight probably being the Clonmel Oils Chase. The race in November 2003 saw a titanic battle between the home-trained Beef or Salmon, who was just pipped by the English raider, Edredon Bleu.

One of the biggest problems that I have faced at Clonmel racecourse has been transport. I was due on a flight home from Dublin later in the evening and it was quite a trek back to Dublin via Kilkenny; this was before the advent of the extended motorway system in Ireland. It was necessary to go through Carlow (now thankfully by-passed) and then onto the N7 past Naas. The drive did not concern me as much as the state of the car park. I had left my hire car on the nearest equivalent to grass in the car park, which was basically a sea of mud. I was leaving before the final bumper race and just revved up the car. For what seemed an eternity, it did eventually slide out of the mud showering an avalanche of muck on the car parked behind me! It may seem somewhat unreasonable to behave in so unsocial a manner but most cars in rural Ireland are covered in mud and there is little evidence that car washes serve much purpose there, unlike on this side of the Irish Channel where many owners regularly book in their vehicles for a car wash.

A day at Clonmel was typical of Irish racing, with a well-informed crowd of hardy race-goers. There was wet ground meaning that horses came back plastered in mud to be enthusiastically washed down by their stable lads and lasses, while the jockeys returned with mud-spattered faces, except where their goggles had kept a clean patch around their eyes. There is also a distinct lack of formality with seemingly everybody dressed in clothing suitable for a walk in the countryside and the fact that most spectators were there for the racing – and not to dress up to socialise and spend the day drinking champagne in a posh box as might be the case at Ascot.

I should mention how much quicker the drive now is from Dublin down to

Clonmel with the new motorway, which runs from Dublin past Carlow and Kilkenny, and then down to Waterford. However, the suggested route to the course is now the M7 and then the M8 rather than the M9; this takes you to a junction about 10 miles west of Clonmel – to be sure, further in miles than in the past but a lot quicker and an even better reason to enjoy a day out at Clonmel racecourse.

Personally, I have always liked the name Clonmel, which conjures up images of the real Irish countryside – and a muddy racecourse which seems to be just what it is! The quality of racing is generally good and this is particularly the case with the jump meetings which are all well supported by the top yards. Indeed, there is every chance of seeing a future Cheltenham winner in action. The best of the racing is during the winter months, even if it is cold. You will certainly find out which horses can act on heavy ground or, more accurately, in a mud bath because the ground can get dreadful and there is a steady uphill finish for horses to face as well. Yes, this is real Irish racing!

4

Cork

Through the eye of a winning post at Cork.

The first thing you need to know about Cork races is rather crucial – the racecourse is nowhere in the vicinity of the city of Cork but is situated at Mallow, over 20 miles to the north of Cork. It is a bit like describing Cheltenham as Bristol racecourse or Haydock Park as Manchester racecourse. I may be cynical but, because it lacked a racecourse, Cork effectively hijacked Mallow racecourse and re-branded it as Cork racecourse. And, even more misleadingly, it is described on its website as Cork racecourse Mallow. In fact, Cork lost its original racecourse when Cork Park held its final meeting on 9 April 1917: the racecourse at Mallow opened in 1924 partly to compensate for the closure of Cork Park. I suppose, therefore, Cork residents can feel they have some claim on Mallow's racecourse activities, despite its distance from Cork.

Ironically, Mallow racecourse hit the national headlines in 1983 – and not for horse racing reasons – when a Gulfstream jet, with just three minutes of fuel remaining, had to make an emergency landing on the course: the pilot did superbly to land the plane safely. Over the next few weeks, a special runway had to be constructed to enable the plane to take off again.

In any event, there are good reasons to travel via Cork, since it is a fascinating place to visit. Its centre sits on an island between two arms of the River Lee. Water dominates its history, with several of today's streets having once been waterways lined with warehouses and the smart, colourful houses of local traders. Just outside Cork, in a south-easterly direction, is the attractive town of Cobh with its harbour and steeply terraced houses with St. Colman's Cathedral towering above them. A few miles south of Cork lies the small seaside town of Kinsale, which is hugely popular with tourists and offers a large selection of top-class restaurants; it also holds an annual Gourmet Festival attended by food lovers from right across the world.

Another reason for setting out from Cork and taking the N20 north to Mallow is Blarney Castle, which you pass en route. I have visited the Castle twice now - on the last occasion with my son on the way to the races. I suppose, in hindsight, you must be mad to stand in a queue winding its way up to a derelict castle in drizzle for half an hour or so to have the pleasure of kissing the Blarney Stone. However, you may feel the urge to do so. When you reach the open-air top floor of the Castle, you lie down on your back across a parapet helped by an attendant – having prudently emptied your pockets for fear of losing the contents down the parapet. You then turn your head upside down to kiss a somewhat smelly vertical stone wall behind you. Apparently, this process gives you the gift of eloquence; it is perhaps one reason why I am writing this book!

Having survived the traumas of the Blarney Stone, you can then feel confident of tackling the difficult task of finding the winners at the races. It is a simple drive from Blarney to Mallow up the N20; you then need to take the N72 out of Mallow for barely a mile before the racecourse appears on your left. You will notice immediately an extremely modern set of buildings as the course was re-developed in the 1990s and was closed for some years. It was then re-branded as Cork racecourse.

The redevelopment has been impressive since it has turned a mediocre country racecourse into a much more upmarket facility. The investment has also brought about improvements on the track, including far better drainage – previously, the track suffered from perennial flooding problems. Although not fully eliminated, water-logging is now a less serious issue: as such, race-goers can be reasonably confident that abandonment is unlikely. Furthermore, there are now large – and wide – sections of the course available for racing, which means there is always fresh ground much to the delight of trainers. The course, which staged just a handful of meetings annually in the old days, is now one of the busiest tracks in Ireland with 20 meetings scheduled in 2023: February is the only month with no racing. The meetings are evenly split between jump and Flat cards, with the mixed meetings now pretty much a thing of the past. The jump meetings have some high-class and valuable races, including the Cork National and the Hilly Way Chase.

The only Cork meeting that I attended was one evening in July 2000, which comprised an interesting seven-race card. The meeting started with a maiden event over six furlongs and then switched to a two-mile five-furlong novice chase with twenty runners; then back to two Flat races over seven furlongs and one mile, one furlong respectively; and then a three miles handicap chase, before a ladies Flat race and the inevitable bumper as a finale. It was certainly a varied feast of racing and you certainly would not find anything as diverse in Britain – and it is infinitely more exciting than watching seven tedious races on the all-weather tracks at the likes of Southwell or Wolverhampton.

Not surprisingly, the meeting attracted a good crowd including plenty of corporate hospitality tents, led by Barry's of Mallow who sponsored six of the seven races: Barry's describes itself as Ireland's largest cash-and-carry wholesaler – the race card proudly displayed their new 100,000 square foot purpose-built warehouse. Pleasingly, Barry's still appears to be operating in 2023, having survived subsequent recessions, the financial crisis of 2008/09 and, more recently, COVID-19. The facilities at the racecourse are superb and are very neatly laid out, with the paddock behind the large stands giving near-perfect vision over the whole course. Clearly, modern facilities that cater for the needs of discerning race-goers in the 21st century are required – those at Cork could not be criticised.

The racecourse at Cork is very flat, is right-handed and is described as having an inner and outer course ranging from one mile, two furlongs to one mile, four furlongs in circumference; this explains why so many more fixtures can now be held. The racecourse is sited a mile or two west of Mallow on the N72 road to Killarney. It lies in a rural setting, looking away from the town near the River Blackwater. There is an attractive scenery as the back straight is set against a long, elegant row of trees. Beyond them in the distance, you can see the Boggeragh Mountains. There is also a straight six-furlong flat course which is unusual on Irish racecourses; only Naas, Navan and The Curragh offer similar facilities. Indeed, it appears that the track could – in theory – be lengthened to create a straight mile. But races over a straight mile are generally not the most exciting as any visitors to the Rowley course at Newmarket will know, although these days a straight mile and a quarter course is often used there.

It is well worth visiting Cork races not least for the variety of the racing; there are, too, some big meetings, such as the three-day Easter Festival and the Cork National which takes place in November. The racecourse is now well supported by both the leading Flat and jump trainers; hence, the quality of racing is high and there are often large and competitive fields. You are unlikely to see five or six-runner races unless there is a major problem with the ground; you should feel welcome, too, with the excellent course facilities.

The much-improved infrastructure on the course merits comment; it has benefited greatly from the recent re-building – many of the shortcomings, common to old racecourses, have been eradicated. There is ample parking, plenty of space, a large paddock, stands designed to give a view of the whole course alongside the many bars and food stalls. The new facilities look smart without being unduly pretentious as is the case with some stands at the likes of Ascot, Goodwood, Epsom Downs and even Galway; however, this is a course which does not hold famous festival meetings or host any Classics. Indeed, the facilities are just what is required for the type of racing on offer – it is difficult to find fault with them.

In my view, Cork is one of the most customer-friendly racecourses in Ireland and I am pleased that it has been rewarded with a higher standard of racing than was the case previously. The much larger fixture list means decent quality jump racing, particularly during the winter, as well as decent Flat racing. It scores highly on visibility from the stands. You can see some spectacular jumping of the fences in the back straight as well as having a good view of the cross fence before the runners enter the home straight.

In summary, Cork racecourse is certainly a venue to be visited – if nothing else to see how a modern racecourse should be organised – and you should also enjoy a day of quality racing. While down in the Cork area, you may wish to allow time to visit other sites, such as the attractive seaside town of Kinsale particularly if you are a connoisseur of seafood. The visit to kiss the famous Blarney Stone is a must for most people unless you have a fear of heights or do not wish to get wet while waiting in the queue in the seemingly inevitable heavy rain! With high rainfall levels in the area, the problems of flooding have not totally gone away but they have been alleviated: racing can now take place during most of the year with the chances of a meeting being abandoned now much lower.

5

The Curragh

A modest entrance to the celebrated The Curragh.

When you think of The Curragh, just think of Newmarket because there are so many similarities. The Curragh lives – and breathes – racehorses in the same way as Newmarket, with many stables in the vicinity and vast areas of turf. Unlike Newmarket with its Rowley Mile and July Courses, The Curragh does not have two racecourses but it has more than enough turf to cover two tracks. There is so much ground available to race on that you feel it must be quite difficult for the ground staff to decide where to site the rails. In fact, there are rails in all directions; clearly, there is no difficulty in finding fresh ground for each meeting. Furthermore, the view from the stands is not dissimilar from that at the Rowley Mile, except for the hum of traffic from the M7 motorway which is a few hundred yards beyond the round course.

The Curragh's history, as the centrepiece of Irish racing, appears to go back –

almost – to time immemorial; it has been recorded that the first race to be run there was in 1741. It continued to expand very much along the lines of Newmarket and, whereas Newmarket established the Jockey Club to run UK racing, so – in turn – The Curragh set up the Turf Club, now the Irish Horse Racing Regulatory Board (IHRB), to run Irish racing. Like Newmarket, The Curragh is also home to many trainers: the superb turf available at both venues is the key factor. While Newmarket drains so efficiently that it is virtually impossible to get heavy ground – I believe they have never lost a meeting there to water-logging – The Curragh is not quite as good in that respect since it can get very wet, particularly at the beginning of the season in March.

Like Newmarket, The Curragh only races on the Flat although the occasional hurdle race has been run there over the years. After all, there are plenty of jumpers trained in the area, with schooling fences dotted around both inside and outside the track on the vast expanse of grass. In fact, following the sad demise of Phoenix Park in Dublin in 1990, The Curragh is the only Irish course holding high-class Flat racing – apart from Leopardstown – so it is clearly the centre of Irish horse racing. After all, the five Irish Classics are run at The Curragh. The only courses offering just Flat racing, though of lower grade, take place on the all-weather circuit at Dundalk and during the once-a-year trip to the sandy beach at Laytown.

Unlike some Irish courses, The Curragh is extremely easy to find as it is clearly marked as an exit from the M7 motorway. It is situated about 30 miles south-west of Dublin. To reach it, you take the N7 off the M50 motorway around Dublin, proceeding past Naas where the N7 becomes the M7 and then you need to take the exit just short of Kildare. According to my AA Routefinder, The Curragh is just 38 miles from Dublin Airport and the journey should take some 40 to 50 minutes. Once you come off the motorway and follow the sign to the racecourse, the large stands loom up – strangely, there are further signs directing you to the course even when you are only 400 yards away. It seems odd as there are several other racecourses where the complete opposite is the case!

As you approach The Curragh, there are vast car parks, which you think would be sufficient to hold enough cars to provide a full crowd at Wembley – or at its Irish equivalent, Croke Park. Nearby is an extremely grand supermarket look-alike, which is built out of old stones; it calls itself the Tri Equestrian Superstore and appears to sell everything that any discerning equestrian could ever want – and is especially convenient for jockeys. Closer to the course is a brand-new building, which is the headquarters of the IHRB – it comes complete with its own large car park.

The road to the course winds around the rear of the IHRB building, past the back of the stands and then goes down towards the end of the straight course. At the end of the straight course are notices advising on the use of the gallops and including pleas to keep the gates shut; ironically, the only gate that I saw in the vicinity was wide open. There are also plenty of sheep grazing on the grass alongside the road, which create a minor traffic hazard similar to that posed by New Forest ponies.

When I was at the races at The Curragh as long ago as 1996, the facilities were comparatively basic, with the paddock sited alongside the course just after the winning post; there were, though, bars and restaurants nearby. A walk back to the top of the two large stands provided a panoramic view over the course: there was no obvious signs of grandeur as at the likes of Ascot, Sandown Park and Goodwood. The stands were no more than functional and could best be described as 'tired' – just larger versions of those at Bellewstown. They were certainly well below the quality of Newmarket's Rowley Mile or those at other major English racecourses. Significantly, too, they were inferior to those at Leopardstown – they looked old, rusty and well past their 'sell-by' dates!

I was aware that the course had some minor refurbishments undertaken after my previous visit. But major work – costing some €100 million – was due to start in July 2009; this included a complete rebuilding of the stands and related facilities. Following the 2008/09 financial crisis, the project was put on hold. Finally, the go-ahead was given and work eventually started in early 2017 – but the budget was reduced to €65 million. It took some two years to complete and the key feature was the huge new grandstand, which seems a great improvement and provides a panoramic view of the whole course and of the paddock. Furthermore, top-class dining facilities and bars have been installed. This major project has really brought the racecourse up-to-date and it is now on a par with many of the top UK Flat courses.

In October 1996, I had an enjoyable day's racing when I attended a Saturday afternoon meeting; and it was quite dry, always a bonus in Ireland. I went with two business colleagues but, after a few too many drinks and a rather late night, it took me until the sixth race to find a winner in the two-mile handicap. The horse concerned was Miltonfield, who was a convincing winner in the hands of a young Ted Durcan, later to ride successfully in the UK. Miltonfield obliged at 11/2 and earned me a few punts – as they were then – before I ploughed it all back on the redoubtable Mick Kinane riding a 4/5 shot in the last race. I queued up to collect my hard-earned winnings alongside various Catholic priests before setting off, just as the rain started, to try to find my relative's house in Mullinahone.

The Curragh is one of the few racecourses in Ireland where ladies often take some trouble in dressing up – and certainly for the big meetings when the Classic races are run. It is very evident that you are attending a top-class racecourse rather than a country track. Generally, the weather should be better as the lengthy fixtures list, which has grown from 17 fixtures in 1996 to the 25 scheduled in 2023, runs from the end of March to October or early November. The course and associated facilities were no more than adequate when I visited in 1996 but I plan to revisit the course to see the full effects of the major redevelopment and to see how it now compares with the likes of Goodwood, Chester and York. I sense that it may be more like Newmarket and you only get a real atmosphere on the big days when the Classic races are run. After all, like Newmarket, The Curragh is wide open so you are quite exposed to the wind; it can become cold and rather cheerless so the advice would be to ensure you visit on a lovely summer's day.

Discerning race-goers should visit The Curragh, if nothing more than for its history in the same way that you should visit one of the Newmarket courses. However, neither venue would feature near the top of my favourites – maybe I am biased, as I prefer jump racing and do not find Flat races up long straights quite as exciting! But The Curragh is a lovely area and, unlike Newmarket, there is no neighbouring town. If you go to the other side of the M7 from the racecourse, you will come across sheep milling around on open heathland similar to that of the Yorkshire moors: there are also plenty of areas to go for a leisurely walk. And golfers should not overlook the wonders of Curragh Golf Club, which is reputed to be the oldest golf club in Ireland. Interestingly, you play across heathland with sheep all over the course and even grazing in the bunkers. When I played there, the combination of thunder and local army recruits practising at The Curragh Camp rifle range ensured that it was not my most peaceful round.

6

Downpatrick

Looking across Downpatrick's back straight – with the undulations.

It is now time to go north and change euros into pounds, although many Irish bookmakers will take both currencies. However, you need to be careful if you end up with NI bank notes and return to the UK. On a recent successful visit to the races at Down Royal, I did – surprisingly – back a winner and brought a £20 NI bank note home which nobody in the south-east of England seemed prepared to accept. I was advised to take it to my bank and exchange it. So, I went into HSBC in Tunbridge Wells, which had no bank counters but about four desks for customer meetings on one side of the room with cash machines on the other. I asked to exchange it but was told that HSBC did not keep cash these days on the premises – a strange admission from a massive retail bank.

Downpatrick racecourse is easy to find as it is on the left-hand side of the A25, approximately one mile outside the town if you are driving west towards Newry.

If you are coming from Belfast, you will approach the town on the A7 passing a sculpture – of highly questionable merit – at the side of the road. After the sign welcoming you to the ancient city of Down, you should then take the A25 and thereby avoid Downpatrick town centre.

Downpatrick is a busy market town with an attractive and historic centre. But the roads are narrow and, not surprisingly, it is congested and crying out for a by-pass: traffic queues start to form on the A7 well outside the town. The best advice is to approach from the west and then you can avoid the town centre, pleasant though it may be. If you are coming from Dublin or elsewhere from the RoI, you will arrive this way via the Newry by-pass. You should then take the N25, which goes first through the rather grim-looking town of Rathfriland and then through Castlewellan, which is somewhat more attractive: it is not a fast road and is very different from the M1 and A1 from Dublin to Newry!

When I went to the races there in October 1996, it was merely a question of turning off the A25 into a field. I am interested to see the racecourse address is listed as 24 Ballydugan Road, Downpatrick. I am not sure where the neighbours at 22 and 26 Ballydugan Road are located because there is no obvious sign of them! The track into the field was straight uphill; at its top, the back of the stand was visible and there was a small building housing a turn-stile. On a subsequent visit in late 2008, I noticed that the entrance had been transformed - with large gates and a drive-way bordered by plants and bushes, more reminiscent of an upmarket country hotel.

Once you have parked your car for the afternoon's sport, you enter the course – and what a sight to behold. There is something magical about the lay-out of the course and it appealed to me straight away. The track is unbelievably narrow but somehow manages to accommodate both hurdles and steeplechase fences. They still manage to run races with 15 or so runners there. The other amazing feature of the course is the extent of the undulations – I have never seen a course with so many humps and hollows, which make it more reminiscent of a motor-bike scrambling track.

The racecourse is listed as being a mile and a quarter round, undulating and tight, which is putting it mildly. The horses are rarely on a straight line for more than a few hundred yards as there are no straight sections – nor are they on level ground for long. After the winning post, the ground drops down sharply before meeting a tight right–hand bend where the horses generally race uphill with a few roller-coaster bumps and hollows. Then they reach the top of the hill before swinging behind a farm and dropping down another hill with dense woods beyond the rails. The last two obstacles are both taken as the course is bearing to the right. After the last jump, there is another steep hill and bend. And the horses pass the post where the course appears to be barely 10 yards wide.

The final climb to the winning post must be the steepest around and is surely more severe than the climb into the home straight at Hexham, which has always seemed the most challenging in Britain. The contours of Downpatrick do make it fascinating and provide a real throw-back to the old days of quirky courses, many of which have been superseded by all-weather tracks with symmetrical shapes and perfectly flat ground. Downpatrick is a course oozing character and reminds me of my youth when I used to go to the now defunct track at Wye, near Ashford, in Kent. The track was in the middle of a farm and the farm pond was used to wash down horses after they had raced. The track was notoriously hazardous. Wye was on a hill and the course was tight – it was rumoured several jockeys slept more safely in their beds following its demise in 1974.

The course at Downpatrick does bring back happy memories of the old-fashioned country racecourses with their unpredictability; it must surely be a place where course specialists really do have a pronounced advantage. Finishes in competitive fields are rarely boring on a track like this: few horses are going to come home on a tight rein unless they are significantly better than the rest of the field.

The card on the day that I visited Downpatrick in 1996 was not a vintage one. In truth, the standard of racing in NI during the 1980s and 1990s was not particularly impressive. For some years, the two courses in NI – Downpatrick and Down Royal – suffered while racing improved in the RoI, when it started to increase prize money: this trend was not apparent in NI. Significantly, NI racing received minimal financial support from Britain as the two courses remained under the jurisdiction of the Turf Club in the RoI. Indeed, it is only in recent years that the two courses have prospered with better prize money along with grants to upgrade their facilities, which presumably have come from UK public bodies.

In 1996, Downpatrick's facilities were distinctly limited – there was one modest viewing stand, a parade ring and a few small buildings serving food and drinks. The meeting that I attended was on a Friday afternoon with only six races and it started at the rather odd time of 3pm. By current Irish standards, the fields were small but the highlight of the day was another leg in a competition between Australian and Irish jockeys.

The fourth race on the card that day was a three-mile chase with nine runners, including four jockeys from each team. It turned out to be a whitewash for the Aussies with their team filling the first three places. Indeed, they would have had a clean sweep if Willie Harnett had not parted company with his mount at the second last when in the lead. In fact, closer inspection reveals that the so-called Aussie team was probably better described as a New Zealand team since Tim Wheeler was a Kiwi and two of the other three – Tom Hazlett and Willie Harnett – had started their careers in New Zealand.

Disappointingly, the other race in the jockeys' challenge produced just six runners with three jockeys from each country participating rather than the anticipated four. This race was over hurdles – and with a very precise distance, namely of two miles, one furlong and one hundred and seventy-two yards. In fact, this distance seems to have been in use at the course for an eternity – maybe dating back to when the course opened some 200 years ago. The race turned out to be an easy win for New Legislation, ridden impeccably by Charlie Swan, the master jockey at that time in Ireland.

The finishing straight did look an amazing sight as tiring horses raced up the steep narrow hill although the ground was on the firm side. The spectacle would have looked even more dramatic if the ground had been hock-deep, with the runners barely able to raise a gallop. Overall, the viewing is not the best as the runners disappear behind the farmhouse but it is not long before they reappear, racing downhill with the dense woods behind before the turn for home. Initially, the runners seem to be aiming at the stands on the uphill run-in before the track bends to the right and they swing past and disappear over the brow of the hill to pull up.

As the meeting ended with the bumper at 5.30, it seemed nobody was in a great rush to leave and, to my amazement, the paddock began to fill up with horses and riders dressed as stable lads; some were still in breeches from riding earlier; and others were bedecked in various assorted clothing and racing colours. This parade continued for a few minutes until the tiny paddock was bursting at the seams with horses and riders – while the light seemed to be fading steadily after what had been a greyish day.

I then realised I was about to see a schooling race or, to be precise, not one race but two due to the number of horses. There was plenty of noise going on with horses getting excited and riders struggling to keep their mounts under control. Order was restored, with an official barking orders, like a sergeant-major, calling out for 15 or 20 horses to go out onto the racecourse. Despite the melee, the official managed to shut the gate and the remaining horses and riders were forced to wait their turn. The first schooling race involved a staggered start with the runners setting off up to 200 yards apart and racing for two laps before exiting the course: the remainder follow suit while those in the know watched and took notes.

Downpatrick racecourse really is a hidden gem if you like good old-fashioned racing. Since my visit, I note that a smart new stand has replaced the antique version which I had to endure. It now offers hospitality suites and holds functions outside racing, such as parties and wedding receptions – it appears to be a great improvement. The racecourse itself has not changed for decades and long may it keep its unique lay-out. Importantly, there does seem to have been an improvement in the racing since my visit on several counts – its quality, the increased prize money, greater competitiveness with larger fields and ever-increasing support from trainers in the RoI.

Racing at Downpatrick used to be spread evenly over the year with around ten meetings, including Flat racing in the summer: the highlight being the Ulster National steeplechase. In recent times, Flat racing has been discarded and there are now only jump races. In 2023, there were ten scheduled fixtures starting on 2 April, including the Ulster National, with the last meeting on 6 October. Clearly, the course has gained in popularity and the only concern is whether there is enough space for a large crowd. Undoubtedly, Downpatrick has gone from strength to strength in recent years; hopefully, this will continue. The main factor has been the dramatic reforms implemented in NI now that peace has broadly been maintained for well over 20 years. It really is a just reward for the enthusiasts who kept the racecourse going during the dark days of the 1970s and 1980s; since then, NI's fortunes have improved.

It may not seem an obvious choice but this racecourse would be my clear favourite of the smaller Irish courses. In my opinion, there is one Irish racecourse which does stand out above the rest – more of this later! Realistically, you could not compare Downpatrick with any racecourse this side of the Irish Sea but you might find a point-to-point course with some similarities. Of course, Downpatrick now has some very good facilities, which you will not find at a point-to-point course. And, if anybody decided to build a new racecourse, it would look nothing like Downpatrick! It may come as a surprise but, if you only want to visit one racecourse in Ireland, then try this one!

7

Down Royal

View along the home straight during the festival at Down Royal.

The other racecourse in NI is Down Royal; it is located some 12 miles south-west of Belfast at Maze. By comparison, Downpatrick is some 28 miles south-east of the NI capital. It should be straightforward to find Down Royal racecourse as it is very near to Lisburn, just south of the busy A3 road running there from Craigavon and just north of the M1, which connects Dungannon with Belfast. Furthermore, the A1 – being the main Dublin to Belfast road – runs only marginally south of the M1. However, despite its links to a network of roads, the course is hidden amongst various country roads; it is easily missed. But, if you spot one of the sign-posts, then you are in luck because they are – thankfully – reliable. On my last visit in November 2022, I came through Hillsborough and, with the absence of signs, I took the wrong road and finished up on the A1 again going back to Dublin!

By air, it would make sense to fly to Belfast Aldergrove Airport, which is some 20 miles north of the racecourse. Importantly, too, Down Royal is still under two hours by road from Dublin Airport using the vastly improved M1/A1; fortunately, the bottle-neck of Newry has disappeared with the building of a much-needed by-pass. The last mile or two to the racecourse, on a busy day, could well be the worst of the driving as it is down country lanes, which can get quite congested particularly with horse-boxes – and you need the right country lane too! The old maxim of arrive early might be more than useful if you are going to one of the featured race days at Down Royal, such as the Northern Ireland Festival of Racing.

Down Royal racecourse has an illustrious past, which can be traced right back to 1685, when The Down Royal Corporation of Horse-Breeders was formed, under a Royal Charter from King James II. Strangely, the original racecourse was a three-mile horseshoe-shaped track in Downpatrick; it was in the early 1700s that the present site was first used. So, historically, Down Royal is not so much a racecourse as a Corporation of Horse-Breeders, which holds meetings at its Maze racecourse. The Byerley Turk, who was one of the three founder-stallions of the Stud Book, ran at a meeting organised by The Down Royal Corporation of Horse-Breeders. Apparently, he ran his race while on his way to the River Boyne where he teamed up with the forces of William of Orange and was used as a charger! Few racehorses these days are likely to have such a colourful CV!

In recent times, Down Royal has had its ups and its downs – if you can excuse the pun! In common with Downpatrick, the 1970s and 1980s saw generally poor-quality racing there with meagre prize money This era was a particularly grim time for NI during the period of the so-called 'Troubles', but the track was well-supported by local owners and trainers, which enabled it to struggle through to more prosperous times. As mentioned previously, it seems that, at that time, the two NI racecourses received little or no financial support from this side of the Irish Sea, despite being part of the UK, and little support from the Irish racing authorities. Therefore, races were worth next to nothing and, rather obviously, the standard of racing was not going to be high. More recently, funding has been provided by UK authorities to improve facilities while prize money has been boosted by the Irish racing authorities, who clearly treat the two racecourses as part of Irish racing. For the first time in many years, they are now probably better off, in terms of support, than those in the RoI: the 2008/09 recession in NI was notably less painful.

The main event at Down Royal in the 1970s and 1980s was the Ulster Derby meeting in mid-summer. But the big race itself did not attract many top-grade horses due particularly to the poor prize money. The race is probably best remembered for the embarrassing occasion when the start was delayed for several minutes when several sheep got loose onto the course! This was NI's top race of the year and I cannot imagine this happening at the Epsom Derby meeting but there were, of course, the farcical events at the start of the Grand National in 1993. You can have some sympathy with Down Royal, when you consider that, year after year, the world's most famous race at Aintree relied on a gimcrack starting gate – used just a few times a year – with a long piece of ribbon stretched across a wide track, which it was hoped would be adequate to send 40 pumped-up horses and jockeys on their way.

A significant step forward for Down Royal saw the construction of a spacious new grandstand in 1993, including corporate boxes and hospitality suites; this seems to have generated interest in the racecourse. It was in October 1995 that I attended a meeting when the ground was unusually dry for Ireland. Hence, there were small fields for the handicap hurdle and the novice chase but still a good-sized field for the opening maiden hurdle: two of the remaining three races were on the Flat, with the bumper concluding the meeting. Previously, NI meetings had just six races per day. Nowadays, a seven-race card has become the norm as is the case with many meetings in the RoI.

In 1995, the Down Royal grandstand looked very impressive although the remainder of the facilities were, at best, adequate. There was also a tiny wooden stand, quite near the grandstand, which had space for about 50 race-goers at any one time. I found it rather useful – and unlike anything I had seen on a racecourse for many years. I can only assume it was a long-standing relic of a bygone era because there were quite a few widely-spaced wooden steps to reach the top; it did not look particularly safe but it was certainly quaint and also quite elevated. When I was at the course in late 2008, I saw the major building works in full flow – as even more exclusive hospitality suites were erected – but I did not notice the little wooden stand beyond the main grandstand. I can only assume it was an easy decision for the local Health and Safety authorities to consign it to history.

Down Royal's paddock is one of its attractions. It lies behind the main grandstand and backs onto fields but it is spacious, giving race-goers every chance to have a good look at the runners. There is also a very impressive winner's enclosure, reserved exclusively for the winner. The rectangular-shaped course is large, at almost two miles round, thereby making it one of the biggest in Britain and Ireland: viewing is not easy when the field goes 'out into the country'. The viewing problem seems to be caused by numerous tall trees, various buildings and other obstructions in the middle of the course. The runners virtually disappear for the whole of the back straight and only reappear as they go uphill before descending towards the finish. During the winter of 2022/23, one of my local courses, Brighton, had a major strafe on trees alongside the racecourse, which has materially improved its viewing. Perhaps, Down Royal should do likewise.

The best sections of the Down Royal racecourse for viewing are by the final half-mile or so, as the horses sweep into the straight and virtually head towards the stands before turning away slightly before the last fence and the last two hurdles; they then move away from the stands towards the back straight where they are several jumps.

In the centre of the racecourse, there is a golf course with plenty of gorse bushes to avoid. Unusually, local golfers continue to play on race days which is something I have not seen at other courses – it may be that instructions are given not to strike a ball during a race. If not, I hope Down Royal's golfers can be relied upon to hit the ball straighter than I am inclined to do on occasions!

The racing that I witnessed in October 1995 was not the most inspiring considering it was a Saturday meeting. The highlight was a fine, front-running performance by Pennybridge, who relished the firm ground in the handicap hurdle to win easily in the hands of Liam Cusack; the horse provided a winner for local trainer, Ian Ferguson, who has been a great supporter of NI racing. Otherwise, the meeting's main interest was its variety, with races over hurdles, fences and on the Flat.

Since 1995, the racecourse has moved ahead steadily and now hosts its Northern Ireland Festival of Racing, a two-day meeting on a Friday and Saturday in early November featuring a three-mile Champion Chase, which attracts Gold Cup horses. The meeting has other good-class races and plenty of horses are up from the RoI as well as horses from mainland Britain: encouragingly, it continues to grow in popularity. In 2010, the celebrated Kauto Star made his seasonal reappearance in the valuable three-mile Champion Chase and was a comfortable winner in the hands of Ruby Walsh. The Irish champion jockey was successful again in the next race collecting another valuable prize: but luck then deserted him as he took a crashing fall in the following race and ended up with a double fracture of his right leg – such are the highs and lows of the jumping game.

Frodon, ridden by Bryony Frost and travelling from Britain, won the 2021 edition of the Champion Chase. I was at the course for the anticipated 2022 renewal when it was thought Frodon might run again; in fact, the horse raced at Wincanton instead that day and won. In Frodon's absence, there were five top-class three-mile chasers and Envoi Allen came out on top in a thrilling race with the brilliant Rachel Blackmore in the saddle. She was a popular winner even if the short-priced favourite, Galvin, in the hands of the evergreen Davy Russell, could only finish in fourth place.

Overall, it was a great day's racing and there was a vast crowd, which the course struggled to handle. While there was plenty of space around the paddock, the stands were packed between the races – as well as during them. The bar under the main stand was crammed and its floor awash with spilt beer. But it was encouraging to see many young people going racing and there was also the added attraction of a 'best dressed lady' competition; it was incredible seeing so many summer dresses being worn when it was about 13C and there was a stiff wind! However, the less edifying sight was in the gents' loos where there was a long queue to enter. Once in, there was then a queue for each urinal with most punters still holding their pint of beer, which they were forced to grip between their teeth as they went about their business! The drinking did not finish at the racecourse as there is a well-known pub named Gowdys, which is very handily placed near the two-furlong pole, and it became the centre of attention after the last race. Looking at the long queue patiently waiting outside at 4.30pm after the racing had finished, I suspect the takings at Gowdys during Down Royal's feature day greatly exceed those of any other day of the year

The course seems to have big ambitions. Hopefully, its various problems have been resolved as there was a major issue towards the end of 2018 when there were reported problems with its lease and the management of the course; there was even some talk of closure. Certainly, Down Royal is well worth visiting but you should be prepared for large crowds if you go to the Champion Chase on the Saturday of the Northern Ireland Festival of Racing. There were 13 fixtures scheduled for 2023, with some Flat racing in the summer months. But it seems a shame there are not more meetings given the great facilities available and its proximity to Belfast. Maybe, this is something the new management will need to address in coming years.

I think the main drawback at Down Royal is the poor viewing on the far side of the track – but the sight of the home straight is spectacular. It is also worth mentioning that there were no betting shops on the course so there was little chance to follow other meetings. The upgrading of the racecourse's various facilities led to the opening of the Hospitality Pavilion in June 2009; this stages events outside racing, such as weddings and corporate functions, as well as being used for race meetings. In short, the overall improvements over the last 15 years or so are little short of staggering and make the course very enjoyable for race-goers although the undoubted charm of Downpatrick is something else!

Finally, if you have had a bad day at Down Royal and need to drown your sorrows without standing in the long queue at Gowdys, there are some lovely pubs with good real ale just down the road in Hillsborough. It is an attractive town and seems to be a haven for pubs of real quality, which are not easily found in NI. I had a particular affinity for the Whitewater Brewery's Belfast ale, which I am reliably informed is the biggest independent brewery in NI; you should be able to find its beer reasonably easily in the surrounding area.

8

Dundalk

An unglamorous entrance to unglamorous Dundalk.

Having opened in August 2007, Dundalk is a first for Irish racing as the initial all-weather racetrack. Racing had taken place on the Flat and over jumps at Dundalk for many years but the old track, and more especially its facilities, were looking pretty run down. The catalyst to the closure of the old course was the major road scheme around the east of the town – to the extent that part of the course was lost in much the same vein as has recently happened at Wetherby. The key difference was that Dundalk lost a larger part of its course and had nowhere else to re-locate so the course has been shifted a few hundred yards – and completely redesigned.

The venture, which led to the establishment of the all-weather track, started in 1999 when the racecourse company and the greyhound-racing company merged.

A new dog racing stadium was built quite near the entrance to the straight on the old racecourse. A glamorous stand was also built offering impressive dining facilities, which seems to have gone down well with the dog fraternity. Spectators enjoy a good meal and never need to leave their table as the action is played out right in front of them; they do not even have to walk to the Tote to place a bet as staff come to each table to collect bets.

The new racecourse was stage two of the redevelopment. The greyhound track sits inside the racecourse, with the finishing post being very close to the one on the racecourse, right in front of the grandstand and adjoining dining facilities. The course itself is a near-perfect oval shape – the spur at the end of the back straight for the five-furlong start is the only geometrical anomaly. Flat ground is also a characteristic – it seems virtually impossible to detect the slightest hint of a gradient anywhere around the circuit, somewhat different from the ups and downs of, say, Downpatrick. The course also benefits from flood-lights and the opportunity of staging evening racing to bring in the punters after work.

Like many seasoned race-goers, all-weather racing is not exactly my favourite pastime. I felt duty-bound, though, to visit Dundalk and to complete my tour of Irish racecourses, so it was a visit partly out of sufferance. The first sight of the course did not impress me particularly as I approached from the north, driving down the much-improved road from Newry, which crosses the border to the south. Coming down the long hill – and still some three or four miles north of Dundalk - I was suddenly aware of a vast panorama of ultra-bright lights; the electricity bill must be formidable. It dawned on me that Dundalk racecourse was beckoning.

The one benefit of the garish lighting was that it was very easy to find the racecourse; the approach roads were wide and would easily be able to handle a larger volume of traffic. This factor is certainly an advantage for a new racecourse, as it is built with current – and future – traffic levels in mind, unlike many racecourses which have been in existence from an era when a horse and cart was the main mode of transport. To be sure, the course entrance at Dundalk is very attractive with a drive-way through some very well-manicured hedges. The car park, though, was unlike anything I had ever seen on an Irish racecourse or indeed on any of its British counterparts, as it was constructed of tarmac: spaces were marked out as if it were a supermarket car park. It was a relatively short walk from the car park to the back of the grandstand where the main entrance was sited - but it was there that I realised I was entering something very different. You step inside onto carpeting and immediately feel as though you have gone into a hotel or theatre lobby rather than onto a racecourse.

As is my custom, I bought a race card and was rather dismayed to realise that I was, in fact, at Dundalk Stadium rather than at Dundalk racecourse. After all, what is a 'stadium' as far as horse racing is concerned? I have been to plenty such venues, including Wembley, which may have been suitable for the Horse of the Year Show but certainly is not for good-quality horse racing. My dismay turned to displeasure when I found out that the race card contained the runners, riders and form, not only for eight horse races, but also the key information for the eight dog races, which I noticed started at 10-minute intervals at 10pm, just 20 minutes after the last horse race. It then dawned on me that I was at a greyhound stadium that also included a racecourse.

I suppose you could argue it is good value for money to have eight dog races thrown in for nothing after an evening's horse racing. But the thought of watching eight dog races with the standard six greyhounds in each race, running either over 366 metres or 480 metres, hardly inspired me. I sought to keep an open mind about staying for the dog racing but I knew – at an early stage in the evening –that it was unlikely I would be able to summon up the necessary enthusiasm.

As a new course, you might expect everything at Dundalk to be neatly laid out – and it was. There is a good-sized paddock with ample space around it for race-goers, well-appointed bars and food outlets – even if some have corny names, such as Silks Bar & Carvery – as well as a large area for bookmakers. But it was early November on a damp and chilly evening; only a sprinkling of hardy race-goers ventured outside to see the horses in the paddock. Overall, the crowd seemed disappointingly small for a Friday evening. I dread to think how few would have been there had the meeting been held in the afternoon – perhaps a crowd to rival the modest size of those who attend all-weather meetings at the likes of Wolverhampton and Southwell on a cold winter's afternoon.

The racing itself was competitive with virtually every race attracting the 14 maximum permitted runners. Most of the top jockeys were riding, including Michael Kinane and Johnny Murtagh. Nevertheless, it was hardly riveting entertainment. The weather was dreary and as so few race-goers were outside watching – the majority were closeted inside – there was a distinct lack of atmosphere. Winners returning to the unsaddling enclosure were greeted almost exclusively by their owners and connections rather by any other race-goers. The view of the course itself consisted mainly of the brightness of the track; otherwise, there was just the dark night interspersed with various lights from cars, houses and street lamps – just the scenery typical of an urban greyhound track.

There was also one major problem with watching the racing, namely the inadequacy of the main stand. It seems that it was built initially for the greyhound track. Certainly, it has a panoramic view over the track but most of the viewing area is within a restaurant in which race-goers eat and watch greyhound racing. If you simply want to watch the racing – but not eat in the restaurant – you are seemingly confined to about eight steps of terracing which barely give any height over the track. The alternative is to watch from either end of the restaurant where you can at least stand that much higher: moreover, there is no cover from the elements. Maybe, these shortcomings have been addressed.

To be honest, the evening did drag somewhat but it was concluded by a bumper where there were, of course, no stalls. A larger field of 18 went to post and this made for a slight variation compared with the rest of the evening's standard fare. Very quickly, though, the lights on the horse racing track went out and the dog track was lit up, as the dogs started to parade. I really could not face the monotony of the dog racing; instead, I was relieved to return to my car for the drive back towards Dublin – and to thaw out again. Sadly, Dundalk did not host one of the more memorable race meetings that I have attended – even if it did mean that I had now completed the full set of Irish racecourses. I regret not having attended a mixed meeting on the old Dundalk track a few years ago; by all accounts, it seemed to have real character! There are a few reminders of the old course remaining, including a dilapidated building marked 'sponsors room' and some old stables near the entrance.

On reflection, I think the meeting would have much more enjoyable in daylight. A warm afternoon would also have provided a better atmosphere and, possibly, I would have been spared from having the horse racing being mixed up with the dog racing. Nevertheless, the new track at Dundalk is undoubtedly a great addition to the Irish racing scene and has proved popular. It provides the opportunity to maintain Flat racing over a longer period of the year on a sound surface. Furthermore, the racing surface – hardly surprisingly – has won near universal approval from jockeys and trainers. Clearly, the course offers better-quality Flat racing than most British all-weather tracks, which seem to do little more than keep indifferent horses racing and betting shops open in wet or freezing weather.

You can probably surmise that Dundalk will be a poor last in my ratings of Irish racecourses – and guess which racecourse has expanded its fixture list considerably? Yes, Dundalk now has far more fixtures than any other racecourse in Ireland, with 43 scheduled for 2023 alone. Hence, there is now all-year round Flat racing with the winter months being particularly busy. Who will benefit from this? Surely, the main beneficiaries will be the bookmakers as jockeys cannot necessarily sit around just to ride at one meeting a week when there are opportunities overseas, whilst many trainers are probably putting most of their efforts into the jumping game at that time of year – but it does seem that Dundalk attracts plenty of runners. The benefit of the 43 fixtures is that it is easy to find a meeting to attend. Personally, I would rather see far less racing at Dundalk and more at other much more attractive courses, which seem to survive on a much-reduced fixture list!

9

Fairyhouse

Heading into the country at Fairyhouse.

Fairyhouse is one of Ireland's premier racecourses and the home of the Irish Grand National, which traditionally takes place on Easter Monday. The racecourse is located 12 miles north-west of Dublin but is not that easy to find as sign-posts are scarce. The best route is to travel up the new M3 from Dublin and then take the exit to Ratoath – the course is a mile or two along the road on the right-hand side, opposite the entrance to the Fairyhouse Tattersall's Irish sales centre. You can also approach from the M2 going into Ratoath and taking the R155 out of Ratoath, which has expanded greatly in recent years from being a small village to an apparent satellite town for Dublin commuters: via this route, the racecourse is on the left. It has a grand entrance and acres of car parking, just like Punchestown. Despite being only 12 miles from the vibrant Irish capital, the course is very much located in the countryside; it is hard to imagine just how close it is to Dublin.

Fairyhouse racecourse is steeped in history. Its first meeting took place as far back as 1848 when the Ward Union Hunt held its point-to-point there. It soon gained popularity with the first running of the Irish Grand National in 1870 when Sir Robert Peel was the winner, picking up the prize of 167 Sovereigns. As its most valuable race, it became the highlight of the Irish jumping season; over the years, there have been many famous winners. For over a century, the course was known as the Ward Union Hunt. But in March 1964, when it was allocated more fixtures, its name was changed to Fairyhouse. From that time, it has grown into a major racecourse offering top class facilities.

The legendary Arkle was a brilliant winner of the Irish Grand National in 1964 when he carried two and a half stone more than any other runner, not long after registering the first of his famous three Cheltenham Gold Cup victories. Two years later, his outstanding stable companion, Flyingbolt, triumphed carrying the massive weight of 12 stone and seven pounds. Sadly, his career was halted soon afterwards when he contracted an illness – he was never the same horse again. And, most unfortunately, their hordes of Irish fans never had the chance to see these two great horses racing against each other in public.

Arkle was one of ten winners of the Irish Grand National trained by the great Tom Dreaper; this included training the winner for seven consecutive years – from 1960 to 1966 – with a different horse on each occasion. His son, Jim, carried on the family tradition with four winners in five years between 1974 and 1978, including the gallant Brown Lad who won three times, twice carrying over 12 stone. Pat Taaffe, who was Dreaper's stable jockey for many years and Arkle's regular jockey, is the most successful rider with six wins.

British-based raiders to Fairyhouse have a poor record in their great race but the hugely popular grey, Desert Orchid, won in 1990 with a bold front-running performance in the hands of Richard Dunwoody, just a year after his famous triumph – in dreadful conditions – in the Cheltenham Gold Cup. Rhyme 'n' Reason had won in 1985 and then went on to win the Grand National at Aintree in 1988 having made a desperate mistake at Becher's Brook on the first circuit and all but fallen. Since 2003, there have been four British-trained winners, including Butler's Cabin in 2007 in the hands of Tony McCoy. And he was going very well when he fell at Becher's Brook on the second circuit of the 2008 Grand National. The following year provided a success for Niche Market, who was trained by Bob Buckler in Dorset and ridden by a claiming jockey Harry Skelton (later to become champion jockey), and he started at 33/1. Bob, a lovely man, has recently retired as a trainer and he told me how much he enjoyed his forays to Fairyhouse and

Punchestown – and how the hardest part of the trip was getting the early ferry home the day after a good win!

One of the more amazing performances in the Irish Grand National must surely have been in the 1929 race. The winner was a six-year-old mare by the name of Alike, ridden by Frank Wise, who stood 5ft 4ins tall – he was missing three fingers on one hand and also had a wooden leg! Jump jockeys are famous for their bravery but this seems an incredible feat although, I suppose, you could say he was risking a few less limbs than the other jockeys.

Fairyhouse racecourse has a superb lay-out; it is rectangular-shaped and about one mile and seven furlongs in length. The Irish Grand National starts on the bend after the winning post and is run over three miles and five furlongs, with twenty-two fences – all eleven fences on each circuit are jumped twice. The fences are nothing like those at Aintree and no different from the birch fences at other major tracks – but they are renowned for being stiff. After going away from the stands and 'out into the country', the runners reach the famous tricky fence, known as Ballyhack, which is situated at the top of the hill before they go down the descent into the back straight; this is right opposite the stands, albeit some way distant. The track is wide and is the type of course where riders of beaten horses find it very difficult to come back with a genuine hard-luck story: not least, since the ground rarely seems to be as atrocious there as some other Irish racecourses throughout the winter. On occasions, the track has suffered from water-logging.

It was some time ago that I went racing at Fairyhouse – I was there in 1997 on a Sunday in early December. The main reason for attending was that I had an interest, via my relations, in a horse running in the bumper. It was the usual good-quality racing, which has come to be expected at Fairyhouse. The first race, a three-year-old hurdle, was won by JP McManus with Khairabar, who started at very short odds, in the capable hands of Conor O'Dwyer. The second race saw no less than 29 runners proceed to post for a maiden hurdle with Willie Mullins producing the winner, who was ridden by David Casey. Another top trainer/jockey combination was successful in the third race with Noel Meade being triumphant with Native Estates in the hands of the amazing Paul Carberry: he was perched on top of the horse, barely seemed to move a muscle and just looked motionless whenever he jumped a hurdle. This ride was some 15 years before his incredible display at Ballinrobe which was highlighted earlier. He is now retired but it seems that this was not his decision although he was in his 40s and walking with a bad limp after breaking his leg. Apparently, he was dismayed to be told by the medics that he was not fit enough to ride: in short, he was effectively banned!

The big race of the day was the Hot Power Chase. Richard Dunwoody had arrived from England specifically to partner Doran's Pride for Michael Hourigan in a five-runner race. It turned out to be a bloodless victory for Doran's Pride after Merry Gale, ridden by Norman Williamson, had slipped up and Corket, ridden by Charlie Swan, had fallen at the third last bringing down Paul Carberry's mount, Opera Hat. Doran's Pride was left in the lead pursued by his solitary rival, Jeffell; the former coasted home to win by a wide margin.

Two more competitive races followed before the bumper finale. There were 18 runners in the bumper. Despite the large paddock, space seemed to be limited especially when one horse unshipped its jockey almost immediately after it was mounted. The horse careered around before it was caught – and normality returned to the proceedings. Our horse, Tigger's Venture, was having only her second race after making her debut in a large field of novices at Naas some weeks earlier; she was quite unfancied by us and, not surprisingly, by the bookmakers. We were, however, pleasantly surprised when Tigger's Venture entered the straight and ran on encouragingly to finish third at 20/1, which effectively paid for a large part of the day's entertainment and the related travelling costs.

Since 1997, Fairyhouse has gone from strength to strength with a massive new grandstand, which enables it to cope with huge crowds. The quality of racing was always good but has been even more impressive of late. Its prize money and sponsorship continue to increase; each year, there are now two show-case meetings, namely the two-day pre-Christmas event and the three-day Easter Festival, which includes the Irish Grand National. In recent years, Fairyhouse has expanded its fixture list; there were 21 days of racing – spread throughout the year – scheduled for 2023. The course is renowned for its jump racing but, in recent years, it has held various evening meetings in the summer, featuring Flat racing – these are real crowd-pullers given the large Dublin population just down the road. Such a scenario is quite reminiscent of Windsor whose series of evening meetings on Mondays during the summer are very popular with the London public. The salient difference is that you cannot – as far as I know – travel by boat to Fairyhouse in the same way as race-goers go on the River Thames to Windsor racecourse.

Currently, Fairyhouse is flourishing but it has not always been plain-sailing. In late 2010, it experienced major problems with the condition of its track. A decision had been made to build a new inner circuit to cope with an expanding fixture list. Initially, this new track had been very successful. But, in November 2010 after heavy rain, its meeting had to be abandoned part-way through the card. Subsequent inspections of the track found various false patches of ground; indeed, there were serious concerns about the cost of repairs and the likely disruption to racing during 2010/11. Clearly, it came at the worst possible time given the impact of the financial crisis and reports in the racing press that described the course's future as uncertain: the cost of repairs was estimated at up to €500,000. Thankfully, this pessimism proved to be only a temporary blip and the racecourse managed to get back on its feet fairly quickly; it seems to be very well-placed now. On a Sunday in November 2022, I did call in at the course. Although there was no racing, there was a busy boot-fair taking place; the facilities and space at Fairyhouse are such that they can be put to good use outside of racing. I was interested to see, not long after my visit, the result of a maiden hurdle race at Fairyhouse with 16 runners. The favourite was Facile Vega who duly obliged by 14 lengths but the starting price was 1/9 – an incredibly short price when there were so many runners, notwithstanding many obstacles to be jumped!

The name, Fairyhouse, has always appealed to me although I have been unable to verify where or how the name originated. It sounds like something out of a child's book and certainly there is plenty of magic about the course with its history, its drama and the sheer pleasure of attending racing there. Everything that I have seen there - and read about since – persuades me that it is one of the great racecourses in Ireland. It has all the hallmarks of a premier racecourse with plenty of space, a large paddock, many bars and restaurants, impressive stands and full-sized car parks. Fairyhouse is set up in a similar fashion to Punchestown, albeit with marginally lower racing quality. I should add that its Flat racing schedule lacks any top-class events, unlike its winter jump racing programme which is very much its priority and speciality – on its famous old course, including the very testing Ballyhack fence.

There you have it – top-class racing with superb but not unnecessarily grandiose facilities – and a challenging circuit for racing, situated just 12 miles from one of Europe's most popular cities but seemingly right out in the countryside. If you are a serious race-goer and have not been to Fairyhouse, then you are missing something. Simply go and enjoy Fairyhouse and remember it is very easy to reach – a short flight from the UK and a hire car/taxi for 20 minutes or so and you are there!

10

Galway

Racing beneath the modern stands at Galway.

Galway is situated on the west coast of Ireland and is one of the biggest cities in the country after Dublin and Cork – and similar in size to Limerick. It has a long and interesting history, with a busy trading centre stretching back to the 1400s. Under the English influence, the city flourished but this all changed after the Battle of the Boyne in 1690; thereafter, Galway struggled. It has, though, left an important legacy with a fascinating city centre, which lies on the River Corrib; it runs down to the Old Dock. Areas particularly worth visiting include Eyre Square and Shop Street, where life moves on at a very gentle and friendly pace with musicians playing their instruments happily – inside and outside – the large array of pubs and bars.

The city is particularly well-known for its music, literature and art; this is no doubt influenced by the booming University and the young who flock there from all over the world. Not surprisingly, there are some great restaurants as the sea is nearby; fish, particularly shellfish, is the speciality in many of them. Oysters are one such delicacy and some ten miles south of Galway is the village of Clarinbridge, which is famous for its annual oyster festival that takes place for three days in the second week of September: it started in 1954. Pubs and restaurants, with such memorable names as Moran's Oyster Cottage and Paddy Burke's Oyster Inn, are well worth a visit amongst many others.

Other attractions in the area include the Aran Islands which can be reached by a short flight from Galway Airport. And, north of Galway going up towards Ballinrobe, is Lough Corrib, which is a haven for anglers with trout and salmon, as well as perch and pike, in abundance. West of Galway is the beauty of the Connemara National Park and its spectacular scenery consisting of mountains, lakes and bog land. The only obvious downside of Galway is the weather, which can be atrocious particularly when there are westerly gales: rain clouds travel from North America and unload their contents where they first find land!

The first time that I visited Galway was one April when I left a very dry East Sussex to find myself in distinctly wet and windy weather; hence, I retired into a pub on Eyre Square. I remarked to the extremely friendly landlord that East Sussex had been very dry and that there was the prospect of a hose-pipe ban to which he replied that would never happen in Galway as they only get wind and rain; clearly, it did not dampen his spirits. In truth, it must be a long winter with plenty of gales and heavy rain but ideal weather for those hardy locals who enjoy rugby and Gaelic sports.

Enough about the delights of Galway – let us move onto the more serious matter of Galway Races. In fact, Galway Races refers specifically to the racing Festival held at Galway racecourse that now starts on the last Monday of each July. The meeting was first held in 1869 and lasted for just two days during August. It was extended progressively to three days in 1959, to four days in 1971 and to five days in 1974. The extension to five days apparently took place as previously there was a race meeting on the fourth day of the Festival at Tuam, some 20 miles north-east of Galway: sadly, that course closed with its final meeting on 3 August 1973.

In 1982, it was felt necessary to extend the meeting to six days and finally, in 1999, it went to seven days – I am certain that there cannot be any plans to extend it further in the foreseeable future. To be sure, Listowel also has a seven-day Festival and this must surely be the limit for those who attend every day as their pockets must be running on empty – unless they have been successful in backing winners. Galway's Festival starts on a Monday and finishes on the following Sunday, with evening racing taking place generally on three days although the

Wednesday and the Thursday are designated as afternoon meetings, being the days of the well-known Galway Plate and Ladies Day respectively. The final days at the week-end are also afternoon events but, in recent years, some of the meetings have started later in the afternoon. It is estimated that well over 200,000 spectators attend the Festival, which does not receive the coverage that it deserves this side of the Irish Sea: unfortunately, it clashes with the long-standing, high-profile, July festival at Goodwood.

Reaching Galway racecourse presents some challenges. In particular, Galway Airport is small, with limited flights. Normally, British visitors fly to Shannon or to Knock. Certainly, Shannon has more flights from Britain but it is some 60 miles south of Galway and, for years, the N18 road has often been congested. However, the major improvements in the RoI motorway network between 2008 and 2012 have had a dramatic effect. First, the N18 has become the M18 and runs virtually the whole way from Shannon to Galway. Secondly, the M6 from Galway now links with the M4 so you can reach Dublin comfortably in two hours.

Alternatively, you can fly to the grandly-named Knock International Airport, which is situated in the middle of virtually nowhere, albeit close to the N17; then you drive south to Galway past Claremorris and through Tuam – the N17 then goes straight through to Galway. Knock International Airport is not for faint-hearted fliers as it prone to fog. The sole occasion that I flew there, the pilot remarked, as we started our approach for landing, that 'it looked a bit marginal for landing but he would fly around and keep us posted'. He did another circuit and then decided to land without any further words. He landed, to much applause from the passengers, before we sloshed through large puddles to the end of the runway and finally came to a halt.

The so-called 'International Airport' comprised one small building handling arrivals and departures, including car hire, with one bar and a gift shop – a major international airport hub it most certainly was not. No doubt this is fine for the many pilgrims visiting the Knock Shrine and Folk Museum, which is famous for a sighting in 1879 of an apparition of the Virgin Mary, Saint Joseph and Saint John the Evangelist by several locals. Indeed, this sighting has been accepted by the Catholic Church. However, it does not seem to be the best airport in which race-goers can either celebrate after a successful day at the races or drown their sorrows, if they have gone seven days at the Festival without backing a winner – Shannon Airport wins this one by several lengths! I would add that Dublin Airport is certainly worth considering for a visit to Galway racecourse even if it is located on the other side of Ireland – it is motorway throughout.

The racecourse is known as Ballybrit and is about two miles or so east of the city centre: in terms of main roads, it is sandwiched between the N17 and N6. It seems to be buried in the middle of an industrial estate; hence, it cannot be described as being one of Ireland's most idyllic settings for a racecourse. When I attended one day of the Autumn Festival in early September 2007, parking was perfectly adequate but I imagine it must be very congested for the main Festival days at the end of July. There is plenty of room for parking inside the course, with access to the centre of the course through a tunnel. Once parked, there is a further tunnel under the course to access the enclosures.

For many years, the track hosted twelve days' racing each year. But just three meetings were held – the seven-day Festival at the end of July/early August; three days for the Autumn Festival in September; and a two-day Bank Holiday meeting at the end of October. However, for 2023, an extra day has been included in early October. The course, therefore, shoe-horns all of its racing into a narrow three-month window, with no racing whatsoever for the other nine months of the year. This policy may be weather-related but it raises questions as to whether such superb facilities are being fully used. In fact, it is only during the seven days of the main Festival when capacity is stretched – it does seem a great waste since they could surely race in April, May or June, although the track does need to be cared for ahead of the seven-day meeting at the end of July.

Galway is an interesting track and unique in its design, particularly as far as the steeplechase course is concerned. The circuit is just over one mile and three furlongs and is of a triangular shape. Having passed the stands, there is one fence just before a sharp bend and the horses then race diagonally away with four fences in the back straight. Then, they turn right-handed and have a long downhill run before meeting two fences very close together in a dip. At a rough guess, they are just 60 yards apart and they are renowned for being the two closest fences on any steeplechase track either in Britain or in Ireland. The closeness of these two fences is borne out by the dreadful fall suffered by Bryan Cooper when he was riding dual Grand National winner, Tiger Roll, in 2016. He was unseated after the second last but not completely detached from his mount when he smashed into the take-off board of the last fence, leaving him with a lacerated liver and a partially collapsed lung.

After the last fence, the runners then go steadily uphill and right-handed into the finishing straight to reach the winning post, which is at least 400 yards from the last fence and, therefore, similar in length to the run-in for the Grand National. At Aintree, many leaders at the last fence, including the brilliant Crisp, have been passed on the long run-in. The hurdle track runs alongside the steeplechase track but is more uniform with the final flight of hurdles in the straight and a run-in of approximately 200 yards.

Reviewing some photographs taken some twenty years ago, the facilities at the track were clearly inadequate for the size of the crowd at the Festival in July. Nowadays, the racecourse boasts two of the most grandiose stands that I have seen on any Irish racecourse. The Millennium stand is impressive, particularly due to its size, but it also gives a panoramic view of the circuit, whereas the Killanin stand appears to offer everything from top-class restaurant facilities to hospitality suites. At one end, its design is akin to a block of flats with copious amounts of glass balconies – similar to those overlooking the River Thames in the Canary Wharf part of London. Galway's paddock and weigh-room have also been upgraded significantly in the last few years. Overall, its racecourse facilities are now fantastic.

Rather than attending the main Festival, I watched racing at Galway on the Sunday of the Autumn Festival in September 2007. There was plenty of space and certainly fewer spectators than the 40,000 or so, who attend on Galway Plate day, but I do wonder what my experiences would be at the course with that size of crowd. It is some time since I have attended the Cheltenham Festival. I am reliably told that, if you wish to see the horses in the paddock, then you will not be able to access the stands to see the actual race – I imagine it could be a similar scenario at the Galway Festival.

The Festival meeting obviously provides a great atmosphere, with vast crowds and top-class competitive racing. The highlight takes place on the Wednesday afternoon when, in most years, a field of twenty or so runners will fight it out for the Galway Plate over two miles and five furlongs, which is just over two laps of the course. This race always seems to be eventful not least due to the last two tricky fences in the dip before the long run-in as well as the number of runners on what is quite a tight track. To be sure, the size of the crowd adds to the atmosphere but only so long as you can still enjoy all aspects of the racing. At least one thing is certain. Galway's record attendance will not be beaten on a race day as it was estimated that 280,000 were at the racecourse when His Holiness Pope John Paul II was at Ballybrit in September 1979.

The facilities are such that there is now an extended paddock and new stands, which were virtually empty at the meeting that I attended. There was, of course, plenty of space and a wide selection of bars and food outlets. The viewing of the racing is top-class but the overall vista is rather drab. The course is hemmed in by various unglamorous industrial and housing estates so there is no sign of an attractive backdrop beyond the racecourse. The drive to the racecourse is via a series of roads through factory areas and, somewhat disturbingly, when I visited

Galway in May 2012, several half-built factories behind the racecourse looked as though they had been abandoned due to the economic crisis.

Nevertheless, Galway is a racecourse well worth visiting, not least for its history as the Galway Races seem to be legendary all over Ireland. I certainly enjoyed the day with good-class racing, with impressive facilities and with so much room – and without queues, except to leave the car-park and even that was relatively painless. It was an all-jumps card and Tony McCoy was present to ride two horses for JP McManus, which resulted in one winner and a crashing fall. The main downside of Galway is the rather uninspiring setting for its racecourse but this shortcoming is more than outweighed by the modern facilities, quality of racing and the unique course. If you want the real craic and do not mind a large crowd, then a visit for say, two days of the July meeting, is a must: attending all seven days would probably be more strenuous than running a marathon! However, if you wish to enjoy some peace and quiet, then the meeting in September is an obvious alternative. There is, though, something about the mystique of 'The Galway Races', which have a worldwide reputation so you really ought to try the real McCoy!

11

Gowran Park

A tree-lined paddock at Gowran Park, with stables in the background.

Gowran (pronounced Goran) is a village some eight miles from the city of Kilkenny and previously was easily reached from Dublin by taking the M7 past Naas, towards Curragh and Kildare, and then branching south onto the N9 towards Carlow. Thankfully, the whole route has recently been upgraded into the M9 and the prospect of driving through the congestion of Carlow has now been consigned to history. It is, therefore, a very quick trip down the M9 and junction 7 is marked for Gowran and, within four miles or so, you arrive in the village itself.

Gowran is a typical Irish village, which seems quite clear on the essentials of life. A drive through the village reveals about five pubs, a bookmaker, a garage, various churches and the odd shop, but it really is quite small and not an obvious place for a racecourse. Indeed, it is not prominent and is sited about half a mile south of the village, where the road rises slightly round a succession of bends and then, on the left-hand side of the road, is a very grand-looking entrance, marked Gowran Park Racecourse. It resembles the entrance into a large country estate with tall, stone gate-posts and large, iron gates; there is also an impressive array of tall trees flanking the entrance on both sides as you enter.

The stately entrance does not misrepresent the racecourse, which is very much an old-fashioned park course. There must be few racecourses in Britain and Ireland, which have such elegant rows of trees surrounding their entrance; they undoubtedly add to the beauty of the racecourse – perhaps only Towcester in Northamptonshire, now sadly closed, offers something similar. Gowran Park's paddock is particularly attractive and is reminiscent of its tree-lined equivalent at Longchamp in Paris, which looks spectacular during the summer when the trees are in full leaf, but – even in winter – they do add to the character of the venue.

The Gowran Park track is about one and half miles in circumference and, after passing the stands, has a tight bend; then, there is a long, sweeping uphill bend as they rise out of the back straight. The sight of the runners at the top of the hill, with the backdrop of the woods behind, is particularly attractive: it brings out the beauty of the course. There are neither houses, factories nor industrial estates in sight but just countryside. The home straight is relatively short but there is still room for three fences on the jumps track, which has gained a reputation for stiffer fences than those on many other Irish racecourses. For this reason, many Cheltenham prospects have had preparatory races at Gowran Park; there is no doubt that you need to be a good horse to win at the track as there are clearly no easy races.

Gowran Park is not one of the oldest Irish racecourses as it opened in 1914. But it has gained a reputation for the quality of its racing under both codes. Previously, the racecourse was jump racing-orientated, with 16 days racing in 2012, of which just five days were for Flat racing. However, the 2023 calendar listed 18 scheduled meetings of which only six are for jump racing. The highlight of the year at Gowran Park is the Thyestes Chase, which is always run in January – and usually in very heavy ground. It is a handicap chase of just over three miles, normally with a maximum field – with some horses having been balloted out: moreover, there are regular British raiders. The legendary Arkle was a previous winner of the race in 1964 and two Grand National winners, Hedgehunter and Numbersixvalverde, were winners in 2005 and 2006 respectively.

Over the years, I have been to Gowran Park several times but the only occasion for watching the racing was as long ago as May 1991. At that time, the top jockeys riding in jumping races included Tommy Carmody; Charlie Swan; Tom Taaffe; Brendan Sheridan; and Ken Morgan; furthermore, Christy Roche was riding on the Flat. It was a typical, good-quality Irish mixed-meeting with a novice chase, two hurdle races, a classic trial for three-year-olds over a mile and a quarter, a maiden race over six furlongs and a handicap over one mile, six furlongs before the bumper to finish. Variety aplenty! The racing can be viewed easily, despite the large track and its contours. Impressively, the runners are readily visible against the backdrop of the trees as they turn into the straight – and then the serious part of the race starts to unfold.

In 1991, the facilities seemed perfectly adequate but major improvements have been carried out since; there is now a spacious grandstand, which opened in 2003. Unusually, its ground floor accommodates the clubhouse for the golf course, which has been constructed around the racecourse, with several holes inside the track circuit. I know, from personal experience, that the golf course is challenging, with plenty of water to avoid but still very enjoyable. Moreover, it is extremely reasonably priced as, in 2023, the week-day green fee was only €28 for a round on a good-quality course. So, it seems watching horse racing one day and playing golf – on the day before or on the day after – is the obvious way to proceed. There is plenty of accommodation in the area, particularly in Kilkenny, which is renowned as being Ireland's prettiest inland city: it is less than 10 miles from Gowran Park. My favourite hotel there is the Newpark, which offers superb facilities, including a stunning outdoor infinity pool. It used to be ridiculously cheap, but the rates seem to have risen somewhat post COVID-19.

My abiding memory of going racing on a Sunday at Gowran Park was, not surprisingly, of the crowds in the various village pubs on their way to the races. A sleepy village had been turned into a virtual metropolis of race-goers who then piled into the racecourse. The crowd seemed huge considering its rural location but it is very near to the well-populated city of Kilkenny. Inside the course, there still seemed to be sufficient space, despite the large crowd, and there was no difficulty in both seeing the runners in the paddock and in finding a suitable spot in the stands to view the action. The improved facilities have made the course even more special and it must rank as one of the most attractive in Ireland – given decent weather. You can take your pick as to the time of year for a visit since meetings take place during most months.

I never quite know when members of the clergy work but I had always assumed that Sunday was their busiest day of the week. However, this did not seem to be the case at Gowran Park on a Sunday, as I had never seen so many men wearing 'dog collars' at the races – with a pint of Guinness in one hand and trying to balance a cigarette, a race card and the racing paper in the other – while they frantically did their research before diving off to the bookmakers. I assume they must either have finished their day's work promptly in the morning or held mass on the Saturday evening so that they were free to enjoy the Sunday afternoon's festivities. In truth, it shows the passionate interest in Ireland for horse racing; no doubt, many race-goers in the area mark up their diary or calendar with the forthcoming racing fixtures to ensure nothing can intervene.

There is no doubt that Gowran Park is a top-class track, which is well worth visiting and easy to reach, but you need to be lucky with the weather. The racecourse is increasing its fixture list and is also seeking to preserve the track by spacing fixtures out over the year, unlike Galway. The ground at Gowran Park can get very wet in the winter and the Thyestes Chase has so often been a real slog in bottomless ground. But the course is quite wide and fresh ground seems readily available, although water-logging remains a problem on occasions. Otherwise, the racecourse is being run on increasingly entrepreneurial lines, following its major redevelopment in 2003. Its website highlights various other activities taking place alongside the horse racing, including golf and hospitality functions, such as conferences, exhibitions, parties and weddings. During my last visit in November 2022, I did feel that the old stand was looking distinctly tatty and even the new stand is already looking a bit drab – but it was built a generation or so ago. Maybe, it is time that further investment is undertaken to modernise the facilities, without anything too futuristic, such as Galway's Killanin stand being replicated: it would look very much out of place in so rural a setting.

With the improved road network, it is now easy to reach Gowran Park and to appreciate the beauty of the course – its lovely setting in the countryside and the spectacular home bend, which the runners climb as they leave the back straight before swinging round the bend into the home straight to face the notoriously tough final three fences on the steeplechase track. Gowran Park is one of the few racecourses where it is possible not to see any other houses, warehouses or factories – something that really adds to its attractions. Memories abound of the peace and tranquillity of Gowran Park, which – sadly – an increasing number of racecourses are struggling to maintain in today's world, as valuable land is sold off for building purpose. In many cases, once rural courses are now being enveloped by property development. The setting at Gowran Park has barely changed over the years in sharp contrast to racecourses, such as Naas or Newbury in England. Long may it stay so idyllic – a sunny summer's evening meeting at Gowran Park would surely be memorable.

12

Kilbeggan

A tightly bunched field at Kilbeggan.

Geographically, the most central racecourse in Ireland is Kilbeggan. It is situated approximately 60 miles west of Dublin just off the M6, which branches off the M4 near Kinnegad. The M4 then heads in a north-westerly direction past Mullingar on its way to Sligo whereas the M6/N6 goes west and ultimately reaches Galway some 80 miles away. There have been major road improvements to the N6 as historically it passed through the main street of the small town of Kilbeggan; not surprisingly, the increasing volume of large trucks left the buildings in a grimy state – they were built too close to the road long before juggernauts had appeared. The M6 by-passes the town, which must be a great relief to the locals; they will be pleased, too, that the new road, which seems quite empty, is certainly far more peaceful to drive along than its namesake as it powers through industrial Birmingham!

Kilbeggan racecourse is situated about a mile north of the main street through the town on a country road, which includes a single-way bridge: the road eventually reaches Mullingar some 13 miles away. Mullingar did, in fact, have its own racecourse for many years. Sadly, it closed in 1967, which may ultimately have been to the benefit of Kilbeggan as there are no other courses nearby. Kilbeggan is very unusual in Ireland in that it is one of the very few racecourses which does not stage any Flat racing, although it holds the ever-popular bumper races which conclude most of its fixtures. Although Thurles has had some Flat racing relatively recently, it seems – at the time of writing – to have abandoned it.

Despite being devoted to jump racing, Kilbeggan does not hold any meetings during the winter. Its season starts in late April and, in 2023, there were 10 fixtures up until September: all its meetings, apart from one on a Sunday, were scheduled for the evening. Friday evenings seem particularly popular, with six of the 10 meetings taking place at that time. This fixture list shows how far the course has progressed since 1992 when the number of meetings increased from three to six annually. Racing at Kilbeggan is hugely popular with large crowds enjoying good food, drink and music in marquees as well as the racing itself. It seems clear that Kilbeggan's management has been very astute with their fixture-planning – and they are very well rewarded with bumper attendances.

The quality of the racing is such that the July fixture now features the Midlands National, a steeplechase run over two miles and six furlongs; it is, according to the racecourse website, one of the social occasions of the year. Unless the ground is extreme, Kilbeggan's meetings generally attract large fields; this often results in balloting and reserves being declared on the day. Occasionally, after a dry spell, the ground can become quite firm. Moreover, some meetings at Kilbeggan were cancelled during the desperately wet summer of 2008 since the course was water-logged. Indeed, when I was in Ireland in late 2008, I remarked to one of the locals that I understood they had experienced a bad summer: it was explained to me that they did not even have a summer! It does seem that the going on the course can change quite dramatically over a short period and can even go from being 'firm' to being 'heavy' in no time at all – with a bit of the famous Irish rain.

The Kilbeggan course itself is a typical country track with its own individuality. It is quite a sharp track with various bends and is only nine furlongs round. In particular, there is a pronounced bend on the run-in and, unusually, the runners are still turning to their right as they pass the post. It is very difficult to claim there is a finishing straight as it is more precisely a finishing bend! There is plenty of space around the track: importantly, too, the alignment of the back straight was changed some years ago. On occasions, there have been problems with the track.

It was only a few years ago that the course had difficulty in securing a licence for horse racing because they were required to install an access road around the track for the safety facilities, such as ambulances, which is now a requirement of racing. Having visited the racecourse in November 2022, I noticed that there was major work underway on the drainage systems, an example of the investment being undertaken. I spoke to a really friendly workman who told me what they were doing; he also said he was travelling to work at the racecourse each day from Wexford – a 175-mile round trip!

The scenery around the racecourse is superb with hills, fields and – depending on the time of the year – an abundant supply of colourful gorse. The facilities themselves have been substantially upgraded in recent years, with one of the smartest paddocks you could ever wish to see, alongside a very modern-looking weigh-room and plenty of areas with newly-laid tarmac. The view around the track is excellent, too, as the area overlooking the winning post is banked; this gives a grandstand experience, without the need to venture into any official stands: a similar scenario applies to Hexham where stands seem unnecessary. Nevertheless, there are more than enough stands at Kilbeggan to enable the course to cope with large crowds.

I visited the track for the final meeting of the 2007 season, which took place in fine weather on a Friday evening: the first race of a seven-race card was off at 4.30. This timing fitted in perfectly with a game of golf up the road on Mullingar's attractive tree-lined course where you are made to feel welcome. Despite turning up on my own, three of the locals immediately insisted that I should join them – and were disappointed that I could not spend long in the bar afterwards, because I had to dash off. When I explained that I was on my way to Kilbeggan races, they readily understood and wished me every success in picking a few winners; they also assured me that I would enjoy it and they were not wrong!

It was only twenty minutes or so down the road before I reached the racecourse. Clearly, another large crowd was attending and the centre of the course was given over to car parking, so the minor issue of parking at an Irish racecourse was, as usual, a straightforward task. What was clearly harder was to find some winners on a tricky card with races run on ground, which had firmed up after a dry and warm day: the going was officially declared as 'firm', and 'good to firm' in places.

The first race was a maiden hurdle over two miles in which Paul Carberry took a heavy fall at the first flight of hurdles, which put him out of action for the rest of the evening – and for a week or so afterwards. The two favourites were beaten into second and third places by a 14/1 shot named Florrie's Boy. The second race was a mares' hurdle, also over two miles. The two favourites were again beaten into second and third places by a 9/2 shot, Slieve Rocket, trained by Jessica Harrington: the bookmakers were enjoying themselves.

Timmy Allen, at 12/1, was triumphant in the handicap hurdle before a more fancied runner, King Ali, won the three-mile maiden hurdle at 7/2. The next race was the highlight of the evening, namely the Kilbeggan Irish Whiskey 250th Anniversary Handicap Chase run over an extended three miles; it celebrated the beginning of whiskey being produced under licence in 1757. You could assume, I suppose, that it had been produced in some shape or form for several centuries previously without a licence! The race proved to be a stirring contest and an exciting win for Eight Fifty Six, trained by Michael Hourigan (who had trained horses in which I had an interest previously) and ridden by Mick Darcy who replaced the injured Paul Carberry. Clearly, I was rather slow in not securing a tip from Hourigan, which would have been useful as the starting price was 9/1!

The sixth race was the beginners' chase over two and a half miles and there was a fair amount of grief. But the favourite, Jawad, prevailed in the hands of Davy Russell. The obligatory finale was the bumper, which produced another shock with Maibet, at 16/1, beating the even-money favourite, The Grey Friend. So that was the end of the evening's entertainment, other than the music, drinking and barbecue which seemed set to continue for some time in the evening sunshine; it was also the end of another season of racing at Kilbeggan.

Kilbeggan seems to be a racecourse going places very much like Ballinrobe. It is well-run, has great facilities and a fine location in the centre of Ireland – and has no obvious shortcomings. Some trainers may question the going, which can vary from being very wet to very firm, but nobody can control the weather. Watering is not always easy to regulate either but, hopefully, this will continue to improve given the work underway I witnessed in November 2022.

A visit to Kilbeggan races is a must for discerning race-goers. If you do not fancy a round of golf before the evening's racing, then I can suggest a tour of the whiskey distillery which would be a good alternative. Kilbeggan is a natural venue for distilling whiskey with a pure, clean water supply and good crops. Cooley Distillery was established in 1987, with the clear aim of restoring Kilbeggan Irish Whiskey and the old Kilbeggan Distillery to their former glories. By all accounts, the local Whiskey business is going from strength to strength, very much like the local racecourse.

In summary, Kilbeggan has much going for it, not least due to its central location and the vastly improved road network. Nowadays, it is a little over an hour's drive from Galway to the west and a similar time from Dublin to the east. Astutely, its meetings are generally held on summer evenings, which enable both large crowds and sponsors to be attracted. Providing the course can handle it, there must surely be opportunities for Kilbeggan to expand its fixture list and to put on a higher class of racing in much the same way that Uttoxeter in England has converted itself from a small and barely-known country track into a much more high-profile course.

13

Killarney

Stunning scenery at Killarney.

County Kerry in the south-west of Ireland hosts three racecourses in theory; but, more realistically, it is now only two, depending on the bleak future for Tralee. The trio sit almost, in a vertical line, on a map of the County with Listowel at the top, then Tralee and, further south, Killarney. There are several ways to reach Killarney, assuming you are flying from Britain. You can fly to Shannon and then work your way around the ring roads in the Limerick area. You can then either take the scenic N69 coast road, going west along the banks of the River Shannon through Foynes (famous for its flying boat museum); at Tarbert, you then go south to Listowel, Tralee and then Killarney. Alternatively, you can drive to the M20 and take the more direct N21 to Killarney. The N21 is certainly quicker, but nothing like as spectacular as the N69: it all depends on whether you are in good time for the first race!

Another route to Killarney is by flying to Cork, which is some 60 miles distant. However, British flights to Cork are less frequent than those to Shannon. Cork Airport is often virtually empty but it is convenient to use. Furthermore, there is also a small airport, known as Kerry Regional Airport and located at Farranfore, which is only nine miles away, but flights there are even less frequent. Interestingly, Ryanair and other carriers are now using it for British flights; maybe, it will expand as travel begins to pick up after COVID-19.

Killarney is a major tourist centre; therefore, the traffic in the town is often congested. The racecourse itself is about a mile south-west of the town centre. You need to go through the town to reach it, since the by-pass runs to the east side of the town – it is worth adding extra time for your journey to allow for this detour. You can also be delayed by the 'jaunting cars', which are the impressive collection of ponies and traps taking visitors around the town! There are so many bed and breakfast/guest houses that accommodation should be easy to find. Even so, with the racing on during the summer months, it makes good sense to book your room in advance as the town can be heaving with visitors during the peak holiday season.

Many tourist guides will have ample information on the delights in – and around – Killarney; there is no doubt that the scenery is quite beautiful and the town itself is also very attractive. There is the famous trip around 'The Ring of Kerry', which starts and finishes in Killarney, and is a must-see for those who like coastal scenery. The length of the trip is about 115 miles and it involves a complete lap around the Iveragh Peninsula, which lies to the west of Killarney. You may need a whole day to see the mountain and coastal views along with the isolated fishing villages. Not surprisingly, the road is very narrow in places as well as regularly alternating between being high above the sea and then descending to sea-level once again. However, the drive is not difficult and certainly easier than negotiating coastal routes around the likes of Devon and Cornwall, not least because there is far less traffic.

Caherciveen is the main town at the far end of 'The Ring of Kerry' but, much closer to Killarney, are the towns of Killorglin and Kenmare. Killorglin is famous for its annual Puck Fair where a wild goat is crowned king at the festivities; this takes place in mid-August. Killorglin has an interesting golf course perched up a hillside which – from several holes – has the most magnificent views out into Dingle Bay; it is almost worth a visit for this reason alone, irrespective of the golf! Strangely enough, the golf course has a tie-up with the local smoked salmon fishery, which is on the banks of the River Laune, and produces excellent oak-smoked wild salmon – though, it is hardly cheap!

Just south-west of Killarney is Lough Leane, with Ross Castle on its edge and several other lakes connected to it; there are plenty of boats to transport visitors around the lakes – should you have time to take in their splendour. Behind the lakes are the evocatively-named MacGillicuddy's Reeks which I recall – from geography lessons in my youth – host the highest mountain in Ireland. This scenario is the stunning backdrop to Killarney racecourse, which lies off Muckross Road – incidentally, this is the start of 'The Ring of Kerry'. I cannot think of any other British or Irish racecourse, which offers quite such a superb setting. The lake/lough and Ross Abbey are both clearly visible from the top of the racecourse stands.

Racing was held regularly in Killarney on two or three racecourses between 1827 and 1901, including the present racecourse. But there was a gap of 35 years before racing resumed in 1936. In 1947, a summer festival meeting was inaugurated and this continues to the present day: it is now a five-day festival with the meeting held in the middle of July. There is also a three-day meeting held in early May and a three-day meeting in the middle of August, which replaces the Tralee Festival. With a further two-day meeting at the end of September, 13 days racing were scheduled for 2023. Several meetings are held in the evenings when the scenery – on good-weather days – becomes even more spectacular as the sun sets over the mountains. There cannot be many more attractive racecourses in which to hold summer evening meetings, although Ballinrobe, Clonmel, Downpatrick and Kilbeggan are all quite special.

The course is just a mile and a quarter in circumference and is a left-handed oval track. Each meeting used to comprise mixed racing and offer great variety, but the number of mixed meetings has now been significantly reduced. The course is quite narrow in places but major efforts have been made to widen it and provide fresh ground, which is a challenging task when there are five days of racing in a row. The steeplechases are run on the outside part of the track with three fences in the back straight and three in the home straight. The meetings are extremely popular with owners and trainers alike and races are generally very competitive with the maximum number of permitted runners, unless the going is very firm or heavy.

Meetings at Killarney are also very well supported by the public, not least because they take place during the summer months. Many British visitors, as well as those from other parts of Ireland, descend on the racecourse. The facilities are more than reasonable, with an attractive paddock surrounded by beautifully-trimmed privet hedges. The stands, which look as though they have done many years of service, are not particularly special – the modern addition is painted a dreary grey colour. In recent years, the weigh-room has been reconstructed and now doubles up as the clubhouse for the nine-hole golf course, one of whose tees is sited just the other side of the paddock. Whilst the facilities are all quite compressed, there is still a feeling of space – like other Irish courses – although leaving the racecourse after racing can be challenging, since most of the traffic is heading back through the town.

Assuming the weather is fine, many spectators watch the racing from the grass in front of the stands. To be sure, it is not that easy to see around the track without using the benefit of the height provided by the stands. The centre of the track now contains most of the landscaped nine-hole golf course. But there are now many trees, which have grown up over recent years, and visibility is not the best – shades of the Bellewstown and Down Royal viewing issues! Outside horse racing, the golf course, which provides a reasonable test for players, takes over the track. Indeed, golfers park their cars in front of the racecourse stands precisely where bookmakers have their pitches on race days. The changing-room for golfers also has plenty of notices pinned to its walls for the benefit of jockeys. In reality, the racecourse is barely recognisable out-of-season, as there are no running rails to be seen with only the somewhat desolate stands, paddock and the winning post in situ.

My visit to Killarney races is embedded in my mind, so struck was I by its incredible setting – it was as long ago as an evening meeting in May 1991. Charlie Swan was the successful jockey in the opening maiden hurdle riding the short-priced favourite. An opportunity hurdle for claiming jockeys followed and then there was a competitive handicap hurdle. Two steeplechases, in which Tom Taaffe was the successful jockey, followed. As the sun began to set, there were two bumper races over two miles: Arthur Moore trained one of these winners to give him a well-earned treble for the evening.

On that evening, the weather was surprisingly good and it was a real pleasure to attend an evening meeting at such an attractive racecourse with highly competitive racing – I cannot recall a more beautiful setting for a racecourse throughout the British Isles. Can you think of a racecourse where, on a summer's evening, you can be on the edge of a forest and a lake with mountains towering above you and enjoying competitive racing as the sun begins to go down – along with a few drinks – and still be away from any noise? Idyllic! It really is a course to be visited and Killarney, as a place, has so much to offer and you could easily spend a week there indulging in all the activities taking place nearby.

Sadly, I missed a golden opportunity to do so in May 2002 when Horner Rocks, in whom I owned a share with my relations who had bred the horse, was running in the Killarney Grand Hotel Handicap Hurdle. Regrettably, I was unable to reach Killarney but I did manage to watch the race on television in the comfort of my home on a Sunday afternoon. There were nineteen runners and Horner Rocks was stuck behind a wall of horses as they came into the home straight. He was only seventh as they jumped the second last, but was produced on the outside by the irrepressible Paul Carberry to jump past four horses at the last before going two or three lengths clear on the run-in. In the shade of the winning-post, he began to tie up and won by a fast-diminishing neck at the very acceptable odds of 8/1, which was a very useful 'little earner' together with my share of the prize money. Why was I not there? The simple answer was that I just could not get over to Killarney at very short notice but do I regret it? – the answer is obvious. This racecourse really is a 'must' visit!

14

Laytown

Unique horse racing at Laytown – along the beach.

The word 'unique' is often overused but this is certainly not the case with Laytown racecourse. Laytown is a small coastal resort some 25 miles north of Dublin. It is easy to reach from Dublin Airport, via the M1 Belfast road and coming off the road just after Balbriggan and then aiming for Julianstown, where you go right onto the R150. The latter goes under a railway bridge and then onto the sea front at Laytown which merges into Bettystown, if you continue up the coast road with its numerous road humps.

In terms of golf, the two coastal resorts have combined officially to form Laytown and Bettystown Golf Club. Hence, if you are a golfer and have time to spare, do not miss the opportunity to have a round at a famous old links course with its beautiful sea views. First, you will be warmly welcomed, with an apology if the club cannot find you a partner to accompany you on your round. Secondly, you might be fortunate as I was: the ageing professional took me to the first tee and gave me lengthy and helpful advice as to how the course should be played – what a nice man!

If you visit Laytown when the racing is not taking place, you will get very little idea of the so-called 'racecourse'. Your visit could be on any day out of 364 days in the year because racing takes place on just one day each year – and, somewhat bizarrely, takes place on the beach or what the Irish term the 'strand'. The only permanent evidence of the racecourse is a small area behind railings which looks like a small village green or children's playground. On closer inspection, you can identify a small parade ring, which is used for the annual race day.

Except on the annual race day, the racecourse itself is impossible to view as it is only marked out for the racing and it is literally 'under water' when the tide is in. Even on a race day, the course is assembled just an hour or two before the meeting starts and removed promptly as soon as the runners pass the post for the last race. In effect, it is the natural all-weather track consisting simply of sand without any synthetic elements. It seems an obvious surface for racing as horses are forever being taken to the seaside to exercise, especially when home gallops are frozen. One of the most famous of all steeplechasers, the mighty Red Rum, who won three Grand Nationals in the 1970s, had regular – and high-profile – canters along the sands at Southport on the Lancashire coast.

Many years ago, 'strand' racing was quite common in Ireland but, for some considerable time, Laytown races has been the only officially recognised meeting taking place on the beach. It is recorded that the first meeting on Laytown's beach took place in 1876. Thereafter, horse racing took place irregularly before, in 1901, a local landowner, Paddy Delaney, established the meeting in the format that is still used today. There is evidence that an annual meeting has been held at Laytown every year since 1901, including during the time of the two World Wars, until 2020 when the run was broken due to the COVID-19 epidemic. The following year's meeting was held in November 2021, much later in the year than normal – due to COVID-19. Subsequently, the 2022 meeting reverted to its normal position in the calendar, which tends to be early September – the date and time are very much dependent upon the tide-tables.

Over the last 40 years or so, racing at Laytown has changed significantly in that there are only two distances, either six or seven-furlong races, over a straight track quite close to the shore. Previously, there was a round track with races of up to two miles being run. The crowds used to throng both sides of the finishing straight, which has running rails covering the last furlong or so. Laytown meetings have not been without controversy over the years and a key decision was made to abandon the round course as well as no longer allowing spectators on the sea side of the track. More recently, following a multiple pile-up when a horse jumped water crossing the track and brought down other runners, the number of participants has been reduced to ten per race.

I attended the meeting in September 2007; it was a gloriously sunny day and, not surprisingly, there was a big crowd. Having taken the R150 from Julianstown, the traffic began to snarl up and most cars opted for the first car park – an uneven field that had been rather poorly mown; as usual, this was of little concern to Irish race-goers. Reaching the racecourse meant following the crowds under the railway bridge and onto the sea front and within ten minutes or so you are there. Importantly, there is a railway station at Laytown which benefits those travelling north from Dublin – and especially for those who enjoy a drink, of which there were many that day.

The small area containing the paddock is transformed for the annual meeting by the erection of several marquees. Corporate hospitality was in clear evidence with a wedding-style marquee. Those race-goers involved were very smartly dressed and stood out against the average race-goer, many of whom looked set for a few hours on the beach. Bookmakers pitched their stalls in the grassy area which – hardly surprisingly – was somewhat congested by the large crowd and the limited available space.

The horses leave the paddock down a track behind the corporate hospitality marquee and onto the beach; they canter to the left along the sand to the start. There is a natural stand for viewing the racing on the slope down to the beach. If you wish to watch the racing on the beach, there is an area of, at most 10 yards wide, before you meet the track. Therefore, space is at a premium, although you will see young children playing on the sand and happily building sandcastles as the runners come past only yards away from them. Clearly, this is very different from the old days when spectators and bookmakers thronged the beach and the racing took place much further away from the shore.

Undeniably, the quality of racing at Laytown is poor. With a maximum of ten runners in each race, the horses carry weights normally allocated to horses in jump races. Those running at Laytown are very lowly-rated and you are most unlikely to see a horse there which has won any race of significance. The big stables tend to give the meeting a wide berth and certainly the top Irish Flat race trainers are conspicuous by their absence. The prize money is probably better than the racing deserves as the management attracts local businesses to sponsor races. The proximity of Dublin with the support from its race-goers must be an added reason behind the continuing success of the meeting.

The timing of the racing at Laytown is dependent on the tide. On the occasion that I was there in September 2007, the first race was off at 2.15 and the final race of a six-race card was off at 4.45. Jump jockeys often ride at Laytown because of the higher weights being carried. The 2007 meeting was notable for a success for Paul Carberry. While Ruby Walsh failed to ride a winner, his sister, Katie, won the concluding amateur riders' race. Leading Flat jockey, Des McDonough, landed a double and there was a rare UK visitor – Dandy Nicholls, an English trainer famous for his sprinters, sent over Quai Du Roi who won the fifth race.

I had been interested in attending Laytown Races for many years. Having finally done so, I was not disappointed. It was a very special occasion, being so different from any other race meeting that I have attended. Perhaps the weather had something to do with it, but to watch horses racing along a beach on a sunny afternoon, silhouetted against a deep blue sea, made a marvellous spectacle. I am sure it would have been even more exciting in the past when the round course was laid out since six races of either six or seven furlongs are not the most interesting of fare. But the novelty factor – the main winner – prevailed.

When I attended Laytown races, it was well worth a stroll along the sands down to the start. There were no stalls on the beach so jockeys spend their time revving up their mounts anticipating the drop of the starting flag. Off they go, with the jockeys screaming at their mounts to race and then the continuous thud of horses' hooves on the sand gradually abates as they race down the track to the winning post. In 2022, stalls were apparently used, so the races now resemble those on an all-weather tracks – apart, of course, from the stunning view that you would not see at Wolverhampton!

Undoubtedly, Laytown racing is unique as far as the UK and the RoI are concerned although there are a few other places in Europe, including Sanlucar de Barrameda in Andalucia, Spain, which run horse races on the beach. One meeting a year is probably sufficient as the quality of racing must be about the worst that Ireland has to offer but this is more than offset by the sheer spectacle of horses racing along a beach, often on a bright summer's afternoon. Undoubtedly, I would prefer to attend Laytown races rather than those at Dundalk or indeed at any of the other charmless UK all-weather tracks – it is, of course, the gorgeous setting that makes the difference.

Shortly after the last race, the crowd departs smartly. As you wander off to the car park and glance back at the racecourse, it disappears before your eyes with all the plastic railings being quickly dismantled. I suspect that, if you returned two hours later, then you would see that the racecourse had been swallowed up by the tide but you will not forget the spectacle in a hurry. I do not imagine that Laytown racecourse is likely to change much in the foreseeable future – it is hardly an obvious target for major investment. After all, you should remind yourself that there is not really a racecourse there anyway – there are no permanent facilities whatsoever, unless you count the once-a-year paddock on the village green!

15

Leopardstown

An impressive panoramic view of the paddock at Leopardstown.

Leopardstown is one of Ireland's premier racecourses with top-class events for both codes of racing. Following the demise of Phoenix Park, which was closed on 13 October 1990, it is now the only course in Dublin or at least within the M50 – the most recent previous closure had been Baldoyle on 26 August 1972. Following the closure of Phoenix Park, the quality of Leopardstown's Flat racing improved. The quality of its top-class jump racing has never been in doubt. Importantly, plenty of potential Cheltenham runners have preparatory races at Leopardstown over the big Christmas meeting or in the major races in January and February.

In 2018, the Dublin Racing Festival was inaugurated; it takes place on the first Saturday and Sunday in February. As expected, it produces top-class racing and is held at a perfect time for trial runs before the big Cheltenham Festival in March.

Less satisfactorily, it attracts very few runners from this side of the Irish Channel, despite the excellent prize money on offer. In recent years, Irish horses have so dominated British horses in the major races, that few dare to race against them on their home ground. More are prepared to do so at Cheltenham but, even so, any success has been limited.

The Leopardstown course was established by a gentleman named, Captain George Quinn, and was completed in 1888. It was carefully designed to be a top-quality racecourse for Dubliners and was modelled on Sandown Park. Unlike the latter, it is a left-handed track with a long back straight, with six fences as against the seven at Sandown Park, which includes the three famous railway fences. The circumference of the two courses is similar, being about one mile, six furlongs. Sandown Park has a five-furlong straight track, which runs through the centre of the course. In the past, Leopardstown had a five and six-furlong course running from right to left. Following the extension to the M50 motorway, it has been replaced, with all Flat races now run on the conventional round course.

How do you reach Leopardstown? You would think this would be a straightforward question, especially as the racecourse borders the M50 motorway. In fact, locating Leopardstown is more difficult. The long-standing assumption in Dublin is that you know where their great citadels of sport, Croke Park, Lansdowne Road and Leopardstown, are located – but they all seem remarkably difficult to find. No doubt, Croke Park and Lansdowne Road are easy to find on big match days as you merely follow the crowd. But I have been to both venues on non-match days – even reaching Croke Park on foot was a struggle, until I caught sight of the vast stands. Lansdowne Road is also hidden away near a railway line and, to confuse matters still further, has now been re-branded as the anonymous Aviva Stadium.

More recently, the sign-posting in the Dublin suburbs has improved. Whereas junction 14 on the M50 was previously the marked exit to take, it is now suggested that you exit at junction 15. You then join a new piece of road – full of bumps – and crawl along for the best part of a mile until you reach the course from the opposite end compared with your entry-point if you had exited, as previously, at junction 14. My experience of this route was not on a race day. Presumably, though, it is an improvement when the racing is on, but it does mean quite a trek to the various car parks which are much nearer the exit from junction 14.

In early 2002, I went to Leopardstown races before the motorway had been extended – and it proved to be quite a challenge to find the course amongst an extensive collection of roadworks in the vicinity. Subsequently, I went in late 2008 on a non-race day and left the M50 at junction 14, which appears the logical exit, but I was confronted by yet more roadworks. I did find Leopardstown Road and Leopardstown Tennis Club but there was no sign of the racecourse which does, after all, occupy quite a large area. Suddenly, I found myself passing the entrance amongst a row of trees. In the intervening 15 years, finding the racecourse should have been far easier.

Importantly, there is an efficient train service running from the centre of Dublin to a nearby station, with a shuttle bus service being provided on race days. There are also buses from the city centre but the likelihood is that British visitors will have flown to Dublin Airport, which is about five miles north of the city, whereas Leopardstown is about six miles south of the city. In reality, it is quicker to reach Fairyhouse racecourse from Dublin Airport, despite the fact that it is in the countryside away from the city. In terms of mileage, it is probably about 22 miles from the airport which should not take long on a motorway, but the M50 can occasionally be snarled up like the M25 around London.

Nowadays, Leopardstown has an extensive fixture list with over 23 days of racing planned for 2023, which ends with the four days of the Christmas Festival. In January and February, the meetings used to take place on a Sunday – there were about five meetings full of top-class jump racing and numerous trial races for Cheltenham. However, this arrangement has changed following the introduction of the Dublin Racing Festival; it seems there are now just two days of jump racing apart from the Dublin Festival. The emphasis switches to the Flat at the end of March and racing takes place at least once a month until the end of the Irish Flat season in November. Thursday evening meetings are favoured by the fixture list, with regular meetings taking place, particularly between May and August. This arrangement no doubt suits Dublin race-goers, who also have potential meetings to attend on Wednesday evenings at Fairyhouse.

Unsurprisingly, the facilities at Leopardstown are a cut above those offered at most other Irish racecourses – perhaps only Fairyhouse, Galway, Punchestown and possibly The Curragh provide anything similar. The stands are spacious and provide a superb view over the large course; as expected, there are many corporate boxes, bars and restaurants. The paddock at the rear of the main stands is also extensive, providing plenty of room for avid punters to check on the runners before the race. There are some attractive saddling boxes near the paddock – I was amused on one occasion to read a sign nearby explaining that, if you needed a fire extinguisher, then you should go to the Gardai office to collect one. I was not sure what could catch fire but I suppose a careless stable lad might toss a cigarette stub onto the hay in a stable but maybe it was just a token effort to comply with the dreaded Health and Safety rules!

The Leopardstown racecourse is tree-lined for the most part; the view from the stands is attractive as well as being good for watching the racing. Unfortunately, it is not possible to see the Wicklow Mountains as they are directly behind the stands. The least impressive view from the stands is towards the old six-furlong course, which has now been replaced by the extended M50 going towards the infamous junction 15. Luckily, high fencing behind the rails has been installed at the point where the runners go round the bend after the stands; this helps to block the view of the traffic and no doubt reduces the constant noise.

In January 2002, I attended a Sunday meeting that featured the Pierse Hurdle and the Pierse Leopardstown Chase, worth €78,650 and €65,000 respectively to the winners. At that time, using the prevailing €/£ exchange rate, this would have been equivalent to about £55,000 and £45,000 respectively. However, following the relative strength of the € against the £, the winnings now would have been worth rather more in £ terms: at one time, the two currencies were at parity.

The Pierse Hurdle was a two-mile handicap and comprised 26 runners: Adamant Approach, in the hands of Ruby Walsh, was successful. The major chase was won by Lyreen Wonder, ridden by Barry Cash and trained by Arthur Moore. The popular Rince Ri, ridden by Ruby Walsh and trained by his father, was second, thereby denying the former a big race double.

The feature races were numbers three and four on the card, but the other races, too, were top-class as is typical of Leopardstown. The first race for four-year-olds comprised just four runners, but was won impressively by The Gatherer, in the hands of Conor O'Dwyer, for JP McManus. The second race was a novice chase. Despite just eight runners, it was an exciting spectacle over the notoriously stiff fences: the winner was Silver Steel, trained by former top-class Flat jockey, Christy Roche.

The fifth race was my reason for attending Leopardstown races, since Horner Rocks, in which I had a 'leg', was running in a handicap hurdle over two miles with twenty runners. Michael Hourigan trained four of the runners; his son, Paul, was given the chance to choose his ride and had picked Horner Rocks, which gave us some hope: he was quoted by bookmakers as 6/1 favourite. Interestingly, Hourigan managed to engage Tony McCoy to ride one of his other three horses. When we were in the paddock, I did eye up the presentation platform, fancying the opportunity to receive a handsome trophy – along with my relations – after the race, as well as posing for the cameras and collecting a share of the prize money. Alas, it was not to be. The horse ran a good race and finished fourth, beaten by some six lengths – at least we had some decent prize money for the fourth place.

The sixth race was a three-mile handicap hurdle, which was a qualifier for the three-mile equivalent at Cheltenham; not surprisingly, it contained a competitive field. The seventh and final race was the inevitable bumper, which was for four-year-olds: it attracted just eight runners. The winner was Kicking King, trained by former jockey Tom Taaffe, who went on to win the Cheltenham Gold Cup just over three years later. It is only when you look back, that you appreciate the real quality of the best horses racing at Leopardstown.

A visit to Leopardstown is essential for all horse racing fanatics; I would particularly suggest attending a jump meeting there. The steeplechases often produce a great spectacle, especially with the six fences down the back straight. The race then starts in earnest, as they approach the second last on the bend between the back straight and the home straight. The home straight has just one fence, as they run uphill from the bend, and then face the testing run-in. There have been many dramatic finishes there and probably none more so than the occasion in December 2005 when the hapless Roger Loughran waved his whip in triumph on Central House, as he believed he had passed the post as the winner – only to discover that it was the end of a running rail. In fact, there were another 60 yards to reach the winning post, by which time he had been passed by two other horses – he finished in third place and suddenly realised his serious error. Leopardstown is a course for drama, with surely some of the most competitive racing in Ireland – there is never a dull day's racing there. If you favour courses in Britain, such as Ascot, Newbury, Cheltenham, Sandown Park and Haydock Park, then you will feel very much at home at Leopardstown.

16

Limerick

A seemingly isolated grandstand at Limerick.

Limerick is one of the main cities in the RoI and sits at the mouth of the River Shannon on the west coast, where it flows out into a long estuary between County Clare to the north and County Limerick to the south; it is only when it passes Ballybunion to the south can it claim to have reached the Atlantic Ocean. Many tourists have enjoyed long and spectacular journeys down the River Shannon and ended up at Limerick with its many bars.

Limerick has a long history of periods of prosperity followed by heavy unemployment. In recent years, though, major property investment has taken place, with waterfront views being very popular. The city boasts some fine old buildings, with Georgian façades on wide streets in the centre; some areas, though, do look shabby. But character abounds, with plenty of very lively bars particularly when rugby matches are taking place.

The famous Garryowen Rugby Club is located on the south side of the city and to the north-east is the even more famous ground, known as Thomond Park, where the Munster team has beaten virtually every visiting team in recent years. Indeed, this ground was where, in 1992, the celebrated Irish prop, Peter 'The Claw' Clohessy, managed to take out both his opposing prop, as well as the replacement prop, with his fearsome scrummaging – and was instrumental in his side winning. The wetter the weather, the more the locals cheer on their heroes, who play ferociously; many visitors really must wonder why they bothered to turn up.

For historians, visits to St. John's Castle and St. Mary's Cathedral in Limerick itself and to Bunratty Castle, which is just off the N18 road towards Shannon, are interesting places to start. Otherwise, if you do have time to spare and a head for heights, you should visit the legendary Cliffs of Moher, which are probably a good hour's drive north-west of Limerick past both Shannon and Ennis. To the south-west of Limerick, just beyond the new racecourse, is the pretty village of Adare and its famous Dunraven Arms where many racehorse owners have celebrated their wins. Nearby is the Adare Manor Golf Club, which has undergone vast investment in recent years: you certainly need a bulging wallet to play a round there now!

Limerick is very well served by Shannon Airport, which is only twenty minutes by car from the city centre. It is the second busiest airport in the RoI, after Dublin Airport, with international flights and is the obvious way to reach Limerick. If you try to play golf at Shannon, you realise how busy it is – and how noisy the aircraft are – as you find yourself concentrating on a difficult putt – just as a plane accelerates for take-off on the other side of the trees lining the course. Not the most peaceful of golf courses!

Horse racing has been taking place around Limerick since 1790. More recently, the racecourse moved for the seventh time. Its new home is Greenmount Park, which is near Patrickswell – several miles to the south-west of Limerick. The course opened in October 2001 – its predecessor was sited at Greenpark along the N69 and just past the docks. However, the Greenpark racecourse was prone to water-logging and the big four-day Christmas meeting was often run in atrocious conditions and, on occasions, abandoned.

Nevertheless, Greenpark was a well-laid out track and I enjoyed my two days of racing there before its demise for redevelopment in 1999. When I last drove past, the redevelopment was clearly taking an inordinate amount of time; presumably, this delay was due to the desperate economic situation in the RoI after the credit crunch of 2008/09. However, it was only in 2022 that planning permission was finally granted for 371 houses on the site, so construction activity is finally beginning after nearly 25 years! I attended the meeting there in October 1996 when the Munster National was run – it is still one of the highlights of the year at Limerick races. It is a competitive three-mile handicap chase and Conor O'Dwyer rode the winner for 'Mouse' Morris. That day, Michael Hourigan's stable star, Doran's Pride, was having his first outing over fences and it was also the day that I was due to catch the 6pm flight from Shannon back to Gatwick: Doran's Pride was running in the 4.45.

That day, Doran's Pride had fifteen rivals and started at odds of 4/5; it won very comfortably in the hands of Shane Broderick, who tragically was to suffer a terrible fall subsequently at Fairyhouse which left him confined to a wheel-chair. More prosaically, I had worked out that there was a very good view of the race from the car park by the bend after the home straight. I was already in the car, with the engine started and first-gear engaged as the runners were pulling up. To be sure, it was a mad – though safe – dash to Shannon Airport but it was before the days of speed cameras. I won my own race and caught the plane to Gatwick without any problems!

The next occasion that I was at Greenpark was on St. Patrick's Day in March 1998. I drove to the same car park as previously and enjoyed lunch in the car before racing, including a modest can or two of beer. The car park attendant noticed me indulging and kindly came to warn me that, if I wanted a few drinks, then I should avoid going to Ennis as the Gardai (the Irish Police) were hot on drink-driving there, but in Limerick they were very relaxed on the issue. I thanked him for his helpful advice and assured him that I was not contemplating a major drinking session and returned to studying the runners in the newspaper. Judging by the amount of drinking inside the racecourse, I suspect his advice could have been quite useful to many a race-goer. It was not only St. Patrick's Day but also the first day of Cheltenham, which explained the big crowd; almost inevitably, the bars were heaving.

The facilities at Greenpark had looked noticeably more worn-out than was the case when I had visited just 18 months previously. The racecourse had already received its death sentence; there was, therefore, minimal incentive to use any paint but even areas close to the paddock had rubble and broken bottles lying around. I cannot recall having attended a meeting at a racecourse that looked quite as scruffy other than perhaps at some of the Midlands' courses – such as Wolverhampton and Nottingham some years ago – when they had jump racing on drab winter afternoons. Scruffy or not, the afternoon was ignited by the Champion Hurdle from Cheltenham, which I watched live in a smoke-filled upstairs bar.

The Irish wonder horse, Istabraq, with Charlie Swan on board, was running in his first Champion Hurdle and, as they turned into the straight with one flight to jump, he burst into the lead to go several lengths clear. Istabraq flew the last and the packed crowd in the bar went absolutely hysterical with excitement. As well as making plenty of noise, they jumped up and down to the extent that you could feel the floor straining – I began to wonder whether it was up to the job. Gradually, though, peace was restored but the bar was quickly inundated with customers buying anything available to celebrate the success of the Irish horse in one of the top races at Cheltenham. The racing at Limerick that day was not surprisingly low-key, given that most of the top trainers and jockeys were otherwise engaged at Cheltenham.

By 1998, plans were already well-advanced for the new course, Greenmount Park, near Patrickswell, to be established as the new Limerick racecourse. It is about five miles south-west of Limerick and close to what was the N20. It was the first racecourse to be built in Ireland for about fifty years – although the Cork/Mallow racecourse was effectively rebuilt – and has been well-designed in terms of basic racecourse necessities. First, there is one very large stand on the hillside, which overlooks the course: spectators can have few complaints given its size and panoramic view over the whole course. Secondly, plenty of space has been allocated for car parking, with access being just off a main road; indeed, the N20 has now become the M20 and it offers good sign-posting – unlike some Irish racecourses! Thirdly, the course is very wide, which gives ample opportunity to use fresh ground at each meeting.

The new Limerick racecourse is a standard oval shape about one mile and three furlongs in circumference with five fences in the back straight and two in the home straight, which lie on a downhill gradient after a rise to the highest point of the track at the end of the back straight. The Flat course is an identical shape and no attempt has been made to build a straight five or six-furlong course, which historically has been the norm in Britain, but it is not spectator-friendly – perhaps, this is the reason for its absence. In more recent times, there has been an inside course at Limerick, which enables decent ground to be more readily available during the perennially wet winter months in the west of Ireland.

The new racecourse opened in 2001 and it appears to have been well received by trainers, jockeys, owners and, not least, by paying spectators. Limerick now has considerably more meetings each year but the going can be very heavy at times, despite the move from the old course to the new one which lies on higher ground. Being a new course, the facilities are designed to host other events, such as agricultural shows and concerts, or anything else which is a revenue-earner, unlike many older racecourses on both sides of the Irish Sea although, more recently, some have begun to realise the commercial opportunities that are available.

I attended the meeting in early March 2005 and I was impressed by the design of the course and its facilities. The large paddock is sited behind the grandstand and has several levels of standing space around it, so a big crowd can be accommodated. The racecourse stables look positively palatial and are more akin to a high-end stud in Newmarket. As an owner, I have been into many stables on Irish racecourses – some are grim and some even worse. At Limerick, everything you need seems to be nearby – and there is plenty of unused space: nowhere is this more obvious than in the vast grandstand.

Inevitably, the grandstand dominates the view from the racecourse side and, in truth, it does look rather stark and forbidding. Furthermore, it obscures some of the more attractive parts of the course behind it, including the paddock and the elegant stables. The centre-point of the racecourse is also not the most visually attractive, comprising a large lake which has a fountain that is activated especially for race days. The whole spectacle is rather dreary – the new facilities at Cork/Mallow are certainly easier on the eye: Limerick cannot compete visually either with nearby Killarney's racecourse. Somehow, Limerick's facilities give the impression that they are almost too spaced out and, in bad weather, it can also be quite cold and desolate there given the large open spaces.

The last meeting at which I was present was not dissimilar to one that I attended at the old course in 1998: the racing was low-key but still competitive with plenty of runners. The other downside for me was the lack of atmosphere but there was a relatively small mid-week crowd that day. Limerick really does need a large crowd to occupy its space. No doubt, the racecourse does better both at its major Christmas meeting and at its summer evening meetings, which are followed by various kinds of entertainment.

Despite the change of venue, Limerick still hosts the Munster National each October, as one of its feature races; with valuable events at the Christmas Festival as well, the good quality of racing is generally sustained. There is certainly an impressive set-up at the racecourse which can cater for large crowds – it is well worth visiting. The fixture list has grown significantly from the old days with 18 meetings planned for 2023, including the four-day Christmas Festival and several evening meetings on the Flat during the summer months: the management cannot be faulted for its enterprise. The course looks well-placed to prosper for many years ahead and will, presumably, need relatively little investment over the next two decades.

17

Listowel

Festival racing at Listowel against the picturesque backdrop.

After flying to Shannon Airport – the obvious choice for British visitors – it is easy to drive to Listowel since it is just 50 miles west of Limerick or about 30 miles north of Killarney. It is possible to fly to Farranfore (Kerry Airport), a few miles north of Killarney, but flights there from Britain are limited. The drive from Limerick on the N69 is recommended as it is quite spectacular, both along the banks of the River Shannon estuary and particularly between Foynes and Tarbert; the road then heads inland and passes various peat-bogs before it drops down into Listowel at the northern end of County Kerry.

Listowel is an attractive old town and is reminiscent of a typical, old market town like Battle in East Sussex, which is close to my home. As you drive into Listowel, there is an abundance of small shops, the inevitable collection of bars and then you meet a sharp left-hand turn in the centre of the town by the Listowel

Arms Hotel. There is a car parking area in the town centre opposite the hotel. If you stay on the road, you are soon driving out of the town over an old bridge – crossing the River Feale – which has a sharp right-hand turn as the road heads towards Tralee. This route provide access onto the racecourse, with the entrance being about a half-mile further on the right: there is ample parking inside the course. There are two other car parks, which are accessed by roads just before you reach the town centre: the one inside the racecourse is very much my preference.

In fact, horse racing first started near Ballybunion, which is nine miles away on the coast, but it appears that racing was only part of the day's entertainment as there were other games and a concluding 'faction fight' involving local gangs. History relates that the latter became uncontrollable and the whole event was scrapped, which led to the start of Listowel Races in 1858 at its current site, generally known as the Island Course. It has acquired this name since the River Feale snakes its way around the track. Indeed, the entrance behind the grandstand requires race-goers to walk over a bridge crossing the river. Geographically, the course is well-placed as it is literally the other side of the River Feale from the Listowel Arms Hotel.

In truth, racing at Listowel is all about the Festival meeting in September; for many years, this was the sole meeting at Listowel. It was originally designated as the Autumn Harvest Racing Festival and was an opportunity for local farmers to enjoy the races when harvesting was completed. The meeting has been periodically extended – increasing to four days in 1970; to five in 1977; to six in 1992; and finally, to seven in 2002. Consequently, its length now equates to that of the Galway Festival. Listowel's Festival meeting now starts on a Sunday and finishes on the following Saturday; like the Galway Festival, it attracts vast crowds. And surely, as with Galway, seven days of successive racing is the maximum possible. I also imagine that Listowel, a small town, needs some time to recover after the seven-day invasion of hordes of race-goers.

Reputedly, the Listowel Festival is a real party – typical of the Irish and not limited to the racing fraternity. This is a racecourse where a friend of mine visited on all five days – as it then was – of the Festival in the mid-1980s and confessed that, over five days and 35 races, he had failed to back a single winner but had never enjoyed himself so much. The 'Apres' racing is, I am reliably informed, something special. The bar staff, in the many local pubs, are clearly over-worked as they keep their customers well-watered – or otherwise – while they reminisce over the day's racing and assess the following day's runners against the live music in the background. Undoubtedly, it is a serious session of drinking and partying, with many punters retiring after the sun has risen – there are inevitably many sore heads in the morning, struggling to recover from the night's excesses before the racing starts again.

The Festival has a wide range of races over both codes, with the highlight being the three-mile Kerry National Chase run traditionally on the Wednesday; in the past, it has attracted high-class runners from both sides of the Irish Sea. There are also competitive hurdle races, including a valuable handicap on the Thursday, as well as high-quality Flat races, novice chases and races for amateur riders. Each day's racing provides an entertaining mix and nobody – surely – can go home disappointed at the variety of the racing on offer. The recent policy of Irish race planners is to reduce the number of mixed meetings. Hence, it is likely that Listowel will host Flat racing on one day and jump racing on the next day. Jump racing, though, remains the priority.

The course lends itself to enjoyable and competitive racing, with a track that is about a mile and a quarter in circumference; it appears very flat and the large stands – there are, in fact, three of them – provide a superb view. The track now has an outer circuit in the back straight, which is somewhat longer, but it has enabled the course to cope with seven successive days of racing. Few changes to the setting have been necessary as the hills stand out above the back straight while the town provides the backdrop as the runners come round the home bend by the River Feale – and then the serious part of the race is underway. The only blot on the landscape in recent years has been the construction of a wind-farm on the hills in the distance. An industrial estate, with the famous Kerry Dairy, is sited nearby. While it is not the most attractive backdrop, its business seems to be thriving and it is no doubt a major local employer.

I have been to Listowel races on several occasions, including attending the 2002 spring meeting when Horner Rocks, in whom I had an interest, ran. I write 'ran' but the ground was very firm and I was there with my brother and some relations, who had bred the horse. In truth, their presence was probably the main reason why the horse actually participated. Undoubtedly, he felt the ground as he competed in the two-mile handicap hurdle but came home safe and sound – and very much in his own time. It was a typically varied day's racing at Listowel, with four Flat races followed by a handicap chase worth €26,000 won by the father-and-son team of Ted and Ruby Walsh. The handicap hurdle followed and the concluding bumper was won by the Charlie Swan-trained Arctic Gold.

Previously, I had attended the last three days of the 1993 Festival meeting held in good weather and attended by large crowds, which were comfortably accommodated within the facilities provided. I took my mother over to Ireland for the three days, which gave her a much-needed change from watching some of the often sub-standard animals struggling around Plumpton and Fontwell Park. While there was the occasional race at Listowel with few runners, most attracted good-sized fields, which was also a welcome change for my mother: and I could more readily understand how my old friend had come away empty-handed after five successive days of racing. Novice chases often produce a high degree of drama. Indeed, there was a race at the Festival a few years ago when no less than eight runners came to grief at the first fence which was, more or less, in front of the stands. Thankfully, I understand none of the horses concerned were injured.

By not arriving until the Thursday, I missed the Kerry National. However, the racing on the Thursday, Friday and Saturday was not exactly dull, highlighted by two novice chases which, at times, seemed to resemble a destruction derby on a stock-car track. The fences at Listowel do not seem large but they do take some jumping. The Flat racing was also good value, with the tight turn into the home straight, along a high bank, bringing memories of the sharp turn into the straight at Chester.

For personal reasons, my undoubted highlight occurred near the end of the three days' racing. Horner Water, bred and owned by my relations and the dam of Horner Rocks, won the two-mile maiden hurdle, having passed the post in second place and successfully objecting to the winner on the grounds of crossing at the last. My mother and I were invited to the post-race dinner celebrations at the Dunraven Arms in Adare; regrettably, we had to decline the invitation as we were staying in Killarney, some fifty miles away. Alas, I was the nominated driver and I would have struggled on a liquid diet of orange and lemonade for the evening when everybody else in the group was celebrating in considerably more style.

At last – in 2010 – I managed to attend the Kerry National day of the Festival and it was a superb race, with Barry Geraghty on Alfa getting up to beat Tony McCoy on Dancing Tornado in an exciting finish. The crowd that day was huge and the course struggled to cope – somehow the lay-out does not seem right as everybody seemed to be walking in different directions to bars, bookmakers, stands and the paddock – and there was serious congestion. I was also there on the next day for the big handicap hurdle race; the crowd was significantly smaller, which made it that much more comfortable.

Listowel is a beautiful racecourse and is surely one of the best in Ireland: few visitors can feel negative having attended racing there. The Festival is clearly the prime meeting but the day of the Kerry National might be a struggle for the discerning race-goer, given the vast crowd. The other days are also attractive, given such a varied feast of racing. In fact, there are just 10 days of racing at

Listowel each year, with a three-day meeting in June – the April meeting which I attended in 2002 has since been scrapped – and then, of course, the seven-day Festival in September. The course and facilities do not seem to have changed markedly between 1993 and my last visit in 2022; in reality, there are few obvious needs for major investment. But it does seem a crying shame that there is not more racing there – surely there should be more than two meetings a year even if one does last for seven days in succession!

Wearing my golfing hat, I have always fancied a round at the world-famous course at Ballybunion, which is on the coast about nine miles to the west of Listowel. Ballybunion is a quiet town, with a beautiful and extensive sandy beach. As you peer out to sea, you realise that the next stop is North America. The Ballybunion golf course has become so popular with American visitors to the extent that its green fees are c€300 to play the famous Old Course; c€300 for a round of golf seems excessive but presumably there are plenty of willing customers, even if some locals have been priced out. However, if I do have a successful day at Listowel races, then I might re-invest the profit in a round at Ballybunion – weather permitting – as I am sure my round would be memorable. That epithet applies to the former US President, Bill Clinton, as there is a statue of him in the town adopting his golfing pose to celebrate his visit to Ballybunion Golf Club in 1998.

18

Naas

The paddock beneath 'The Circle' at Naas.

Naas is a busy town some thirty miles south-west of Dublin – and surrounded by the racing fraternity. Punchestown racecourse is just four miles away from Naas, and you only need to travel another ten miles along the M7 before arriving at Curragh, with its famous racecourse and many racing stables. Before reaching Naas on the M7, you pass the rather macabre-sounding village of Kill, where the Goffs Thoroughbred Sales are held. This area really is the hot-bed of the Irish horse racing business. The M7 down to Naas goes past several recently-built industrial estates and many local companies seem to be prospering, despite COVID-19 and, prior to that, the major set-backs to the economy following the financial crisis of 2008/09.

Previously, the course was very easy to find if you approached it from Dublin on the M7, as the Naas by-pass swings round to the north side of the town while you peel off and head straight-on: you should soon see the racecourse through the houses on the left-hand side of the road. However, more and more building work has taken place in recent years and the racecourse is not as conspicuous as it once was. Furthermore, sign-posting locally is erratic; if you miss the left-turn at the traffic lights, you will be heading towards the centre of Naas where it is difficult to turn round.

Assuming you do see the one modest sign-post, you should reach the ample car park – a characteristic of many Irish racecourses; its surface is variable and very different from that of most top supermarkets. One of my visits to Naas racecourse coincided with some typical weather just as I was making a quick get-away to catch a flight. Apart from being drenched in the sodden bog of a car park, I did well to manoeuvre the car out of it. Reassuringly, there was a line of tractors with tow ropes to rescue unlucky race-goers.

Following the long-lasting improvements to the M7, it now takes about 40 minutes to drive to Naas from Dublin Airport – providing there are no traffic jams, which are unfortunately common. All kind of reasons are cited, including horses running down the road, along with more predictable excuses of road-works, accidents or broken-down vehicles. There are several good pubs near the M7 in the Naas area, which are suitable for a quick lunch and a beer before racing; to be sure, the word 'quick' is probably being unduly optimistic where food and drinks provision is concerned in Ireland. It is certainly quicker to obtain sandwiches from a delicatessen shop attached to a garage.

During that visit to Naas racecourse with the weather issues in the car park, I called in at such an establishment, located a mile or so from the course. Unfortunately, my order of a cheese and tomato sandwich to a shop assistant was mis-translated into a chicken tikka sandwich while I had been speaking to the person behind me in the queue. When asked if I wanted anything else, I requested an egg mayonnaise sandwich and continued my conversation, only to turn round as the shop assistant was adding egg mayonnaise onto the same sandwich before I had a chance to stop her! Being late anyway and aware of quite a queue forming behind me, I declined to ask her to start again. I should add that I managed to eat the monster sandwich in the car park before dashing into the racecourse. I survived it even if I did fail to back a winner all afternoon.

Naas is a busy racecourse and the fixture list for 2023 showed 20 meetings in total and at least one meeting every month of the year. Nowadays, the racing at Naas seems to have a bias towards Flat racing but the quality of its racing – under both codes – is at the top-end. Given its proximity to Dublin and the major training stables, this is hardly surprising. Previously, there were some mixed meetings but these have been largely discontinued. The racecourse is one of the few in Ireland to use a straight Flat course; hence, there are many Flat races over five and six furlongs during the summer. In short, there is something on offer for everyone at Naas.

The course is also very wide and this attracts large fields, particularly over hurdles during the winter months. There are often up to 25 runners in a maiden hurdle race and it soon becomes abundantly clear to the neutral observer that most runners have very little interest in trying to win the race. First, the jockeys on these horses tend to hang back at the start. Secondly, they seem to be quite astute in turning their horse around just as the tapes rise and ending up facing the wrong direction. Thirdly, they seem to make very little effort to atone for their misfortune in 'missing' the start.

History suggests that there is often a call from the starter telling the jockeys to line up, followed by a further instruction, 'triers at the front'! At this point, a few horses come forward, while the rest stay well back; many are so slowly away that the horses are well-strung out before they even jump a hurdle. The likely culprits are those that have not run their initial three races; it is only after a horse runs three races that it can be handicapped. There seems to be minimal advantage in a horse putting in a good run before securing a handicap rating, unless it is clearly above handicap standard. Possibly, I am being somewhat cynical but this view is quite widely held; indeed, at least one trainer has confirmed to me that this interpretation is reasonably accurate.

The course at Naas is about one and a half miles round and is flat throughout except for a slight rise to the winning post – and it is stiffer than it looks. It is the type of racecourse where there can surely be few valid excuses for a troubled run as it is wide and has long sweeping bends. Like most Irish courses, the ground in the winter months is often similar to that in the car park: horses can get legless on the final climb to the post and sometimes really struggle to raise a gallop there. Nevertheless, the racecourse is popular with local trainers and most races have large fields during the winter months, probably because trainers have limited options, given the paucity of meetings in Ireland during that time of the year. Many good horses have won their first hurdle or steeplechase on the Naas track, and many good Flat horses have emulated them. The overall quality of racing is generally of a high standard: races at Naas do take some winning.

I have quite an affinity with Naas races; it was my first taste of Irish racing. Over the years, I have attended several meetings there, including the first time that I had an interest in a horse running. In general terms, the racecourse is not particularly colourful. It has a large, almost triangular-shaped, paddock which is very functional with a trimmed hedge and a few flowers. Importantly, it can readily handle big fields and the consequentially large collection of owners, trainers and jockeys: its paddock area is probably the best feature of the racecourse. However, I was pleased to see some notable improvements on my last visit to the course on the final day of the Irish Flat racing season in November 2022. Despite a wild hailstorm at one point, I had a thoroughly enjoyable afternoon.

I noticed, too, the Opera Hat Bar, which overlooks the paddock and used to have four tree stumps outside that had been converted into tables, had been both re-vamped and re-branded as 'The Post'. It served hot meals but, in truth, the eating-area reminded me of a school canteen as customers queued, with a tray, and then found a table at which to eat their meals. More impressive was a round building next to the paddock known, perhaps inevitably, as 'The Circle'. I did not have an opportunity to experience it since 'The Circle' was specifically reserved for owners and trainers – there was certainly nothing like that, when I was a part-owner with a runner in 1997!

In the past, there were four stands of different shapes and sizes, which – at best – could be described as adequate, but they were more reminiscent of stands at lower league football grounds. They did not look modern but did provide the basic requirements of shelter and a good view of the racecourse, along with the odd bar and Tote facilities. I was pleased to note their replacement by a new good-quality stand; there was a large area beneath it with TV screens, betting facilities, bars and dining-rooms, all of which the average race-goer requires in today's hospitality world.

Overall, the improvements bring many benefits; no longer does the course look cheerless on a drab November afternoon. The racecourse still seems reasonably popular. I noted one optimist, an ice-cream seller in his van. Hardly surprisingly, trade appeared to be slow – very slow. Many race-goers spent the afternoon huddled inside, either venturing out occasionally to the paddock or to watch the racing from the stands since the weather was unpredictable. I did note that the staff at the racecourse tried hard to be welcoming, whether they were race card sellers, tractor drivers in the car park – poised to tow out stranded motorists – and even the staff in the Tote building, who wish you good luck when you place a bet with them.

Naas racecourse undoubtedly has good racing to offer. Initially, I thought it targeted racing aficionados during the wet winter months – unless you strike lucky and pick a fine day. It did not seem to be a racecourse to which you should take your wife or girlfriend – assuming they are occasional race-goers – during the winter. However, I believe this viewpoint no longer applies, although you still need to be prepared for the mud in the car park and the likely wet weather at the racecourse. But the facilities at Naas are such that you can have an enjoyable day whatever the weather. Of course, an evening meeting during the summer should normally see the racecourse at its best.

As a town, Naas has much to offer with good accommodation, fine restaurants and a considerable number of pubs. In fact, the locals are probably more racing-orientated when the horse racing is on at nearby Punchestown and particularly during the Festival in April: by comparison, the meetings at Naas are lower profile. And, to an extent, Naas racecourse lives in the shadow of Punchestown racecourse, which has gone from strength to strength in recent years; Naas might also be adversely impacted by the new Flat course being constructed there. Nevertheless, the recent improvements bring clear benefits, not least the fact that the quality of racing at Naas has risen of late as well as being highly competitive, due in part to the big fields that it attracts.

For some years, I believed that the racecourse at Naas could have done with a face-lift and either be effectively re-built, like Cork/Mallow; alternatively, commissioning a new grandstand – instead of retaining several old, drab buildings – would have been an obvious option. Pleasingly, this latter option has been adopted, with a new grandstand now in place. At a general level, only modest investment – with a few notable exceptions – has been undertaken at Irish racecourses since I first went racing in Ireland in the early 1990s. Naas is certainly one of the exceptions – it has progressed from being tired and old to becoming a racecourse which is both more customer-friendly and more pleasing on the eye for the discerning race-goer.

19

Navan

Threatening skies over Navan's paddock.

Aside from their distance from Dublin and its Airport, Navan and Naas have other similarities. Navan is located to the north-west of Dublin and can be quite easily reached via the N3, now M3. The two racecourses are broadly the same size; both have a six-furlong straight track for Flat racing and both stage a similar amount of racing. Navan had two less meetings than Naas scheduled for 2023. Navan has a slight bias towards jumping; for Naas, the reverse is true. In terms of shape, Navan's track is more of an oval, whereas that of Naas is squarer; in fact, Navan's track is very similar in shape to that of Newbury. However, Navan's back straight is steadily downhill, which gives rise to a testing uphill finish, although there is a downhill section at the beginning of the long home straight.

The racecourse at Navan is sited in Proudstown Park – the course operated under that name until 1951. Navan is a busy market town and, despite the opening of the M3, traffic levels have not declined in the town centre. With several busy ring roads nearby, the racecourse is not easy to find but you need to follow the sign-posts, which are generally good. It is located about a mile or so north of the town, on the left side of the R162. This road is not a major by-way: most race-goers will probably drive through the town to access the R162 and you should allow extra time for congestion, particularly on a Saturday.

Navan is situated on the River Boyne and it is only a short drive east, along the N51 to Slane and beyond towards Drogheda via the Boyne valley, to locate the site of the Battle of the Boyne, which famously took place on 1 July 1690. It is just 12 miles or so from Navan to the M1 junction, near Drogheda, which provides an easy connection to NI, as well as being relatively close to the sandy beaches, including Laytown – with its racecourse on the beach – and nearby Bettystown.

Previously, racecourse facilities at Navan, with their open spaces, compared very favourably with those at Naas. However, following recent investment at Naas, this gap has closed. At Navan, there is one large stand, which is beginning to look dated, but it offers a commanding view of the racecourse and its surrounding countryside. Beyond the stand, is a panoramic restaurant, which previously doubled up as part of the sadly now defunct golf club. The paddock is extensive and is sited in an area, with acres of space for race-goers to mingle; indeed, the whole set-up provides relative comfort, even in bad weather. Overall, the racecourse seems to be well-maintained; there are few signs of paint flaking from the walls, holes in the ground and cracked glass, etc. The most recent improvement appears to be the presentation area – for winning owners – in the middle of the paddock.

The track at Navan must be one of the widest anywhere in Britain or Ireland, which means fresh ground is regularly available and large fields are attracted. Furthermore, it is arguably one of the fairest tracks given its extensive space and a long back straight. Jockeys are unlikely to elicit much sympathy if they claim they were boxed in or, even worse, brought down. Both the hurdles and fences are wide and jockeys have ample opportunity to provide their mounts with a clear view of the obstacle.

Interestingly, Navan seems able to accommodate up to 30 runners in a maiden hurdle, rather than the estimated 25 or so runners at Naas. In the former case, close to 25 runners may well be there solely for the exercise, as the starter's refrain – 'line up jockeys, triers at the front' is heard once again! Hence, around five horses generally congregate at the front, with the remainder scattered around the starting area. Some evidence of this practice is provided by the betting for a typical 30-runner maiden – an even-money or odds-on favourite is not unusual in such a race. Furthermore, these short-priced favourites often live up to expectation and win, although – in such a large field of inexperienced horses – you might think there was every chance of them getting into trouble on the way round. In fact, the five or so seriously interested horses run their own race ahead of the other 25 or so, who are behind virtually from the start: hence, an official 30-runner race very soon becomes a five-runner affair.

The quality of the jump racing at Navan is near the top and probably only surpassed by Punchestown, Fairyhouse and Leopardstown at their big meetings; the steeplechase track is particularly favoured by the top trainers for their novice chasers. Plenty of Cheltenham Festival winners have won at Navan; often, it is their first win over fences while others have had their key preparatory races there before the big meetings. Flat racing at Navan is of a lower quality, although it does attract some good horses running in maiden and juvenile races: top Irish Flat racing trainers still bring valuable horses to the racecourse.

The first meeting that I attended, in 1995, at Navan was a lacklustre affair. The Flat racing card that day did not provide inspiring memories for me, since it consisted of maiden races, low-grade handicaps and a concluding bumper, by which time the weather had deteriorated. But Navan did leave a lasting impression of a top-quality racecourse with good facilities and fine viewing, despite the size of the track, set against a very pleasant backdrop with tall trees both down the back straight and around the long sweeping bend into the finishing straight. This viewpoint contrasted with the comparatively dreary surroundings at Naas.

For 2023, there were 18 days' racing scheduled at Navan, of which nine were for jumping enthusiasts – with regular racing between November and February – and nine were on the Flat. Previously, the racecourse retained a period of at least three months – between late June and late September – with no fixtures. Now, the calendar is similar to that of Naas in that Navan stages races during every month of the year. Undoubtedly, it is the long-distance chases that are a hallmark of its winter racing; they comprise some of the most valuable races held at the track. Clearly, only an honest three-mile staying chaser will last out Navan's punishing home straight when the going is bottomless in the depths of winter; this explains why the racecourse is so popular with local trainers.

In December 2009, I attended a meeting there, which included a competitive three-mile chase. The finish was typical of one associated with Navan, with only the really game horses lasting home on the punishing uphill climb to the post. The most valuable race of the day was a four-runner affair over hurdles worth just under €50,000 to the winner, which shows that there is some serious prize money to be won at the track. The weather was very sunny for December but it was cold. Somewhat worryingly, there was just a small crowd for a top-quality card on a Sunday afternoon; this provided the first inkling that I had experienced of the adverse impact of the recession on the Irish racing scene. For enthusiasts of jumping, you could not have wished for much better racing on a high-quality course and a fine day – yet where was everyone?

I also attended Navan for a jumping meeting on a Saturday in March 2017. Again, the crowd seemed sparse, given both the quality of the racing and the fact that it is located close to Dublin. I cannot recall precisely, but Ireland may have been playing in the Six Nations Rugby tournament that day; if that were the case, it would have been a major distraction from the racing!

In the past, the racecourse was open not just for its 18 days of horse racing each year, but also to accommodate the now closed Navan Golf Club. The reasons for its closure are not clear but the financial crisis of 2008/09 may well have been a key factor. Previously, there had been nine holes inside the racecourse and nine outside it, along with a large driving range. When I played there quite some time ago, the staff in the office were very helpful, including the redoubtable Sheila who could find you clubs, shoes and a starting time with the minimum of fuss!

On a sunny evening, the course was enjoyable to play, although some holes inside the racecourse were rather mundane. When I was on the golf course, the large size of the racecourse became very apparent. However, it was somewhat disconcerting that, when you pulled a ball slightly and it disappeared onto the racecourse just short of the open ditch – and with a good lie – you found yourself out of bounds. Another highlight of the golf course was the superb bar and restaurant to which you could retire after your round, eating and drinking in some comfort. It sits upstairs about a furlong beyond the winning post and offers a panoramic view over the whole course. Nowadays, this restaurant appears to be for the sole use of the racecourse.

The closure of the golf course has given way to the building of the Navan Adventure Centre for Children. In all honesty, it looks quite scruffy and nothing like as attractive as the golf course. Presumably, it runs at a profit, perhaps with the help of subsidies, whereas the golf course did not appear to do so. The former golf driving range is now totally dedicated to parking for the racecourse. Overall, it is a great shame that the golf course has closed, not least as it enhanced the view of the racecourse and its surroundings.

Navan racecourse reminds me not only of Newbury but also of Sandown Park, due to the extended width of the track and the quality of the stands and associated bars; of course, it is not on the scale of these two English courses. The quality of its racing, though, is as good as anything offered at Newbury or Sandown Park, except perhaps that Navan's Flat racing is rather lower-grade with virtually no valuable races. Hence, the racecourse will particularly appeal to those who prefer top-quality jump racing courses rather than those simply seeking a more rural environment.

In my view, Navan is a 'must' to visit and this can readily be achieved in a day-trip from Britain, given its proximity to Dublin Airport. Despite the new M3, it is still necessary to navigate through an often-congested Navan, for which extra time should be allowed. Presumably, there is a better way to reach the racecourse and avoid the middle of the town, but I have yet to find it.

For serious race-goers, attending one of Navan's major winter meetings should be a priority. But, if you are undertaking a day-trip, the weather can be problematic, with the risk of abandonment through either water-logging or frost. I should add that, if you are seeking low-cost flights, you often need to book several weeks ahead. If all else fails, then there are many other attractions in the RoI, and particularly in Dublin. I can particularly recommend a visit to the Guinness Brewery in Dublin, which I exchanged for a day's racing at Naas, as the horse, in which I had a share, was pulled out of its planned race at late notice. Yes, the Guinness trip was certainly memorable – and Guinness is good for you!

20

Punchestown

Spacious paddock area at classy Punchestown.

It is not for nothing that Punchestown is known as 'Peerless' Punchestown. Indeed, a book under this very title was published in 2004 to celebrate 150 years of racing at the famous racecourse, which is just four miles by road from Naas; that fact highlights one of its few drawbacks, namely, access to the track. The Festival meeting is held at the end of April and now runs to five days. Having turned left just after Naas racecourse, it can be a tortuous drive actually to enter the racecourse. While officials have worked hard to improve matters, the major issue is the success story of the Festival and the huge crowds that it generates. The many narrow country lanes around the course have to absorb a vast increase in traffic and can barely cope. Are Cheltenham, Epsom Downs, Glorious Goodwood or Royal Ascot any better on their big days? Once you reach the racecourse itself, parking is no problem as there are acres of ground – the only problem is finding your car at the end of the day!

As for the racecourse itself and everything associated with it, the epithet of 'peerless' is well-chosen. Of all the racecourses that I have visited, including those in Britain and Ireland, along with some 20 that I have visited outside the British Isles, it is indisputably my Number One. To be sure, Longchamp is a beautiful racecourse; Ascot is similar with superb stands; and Aintree is very special – not least for the sheer drama of the Grand National – but Punchestown has all these qualities as well as being friendly and it also offers a lovely rural setting.

Punchestown's first meeting in 1854 was over stone walls and large banks. Its duration was just two days and it was only some 10 years later that fences and hurdles were introduced. The famous Bank course has been maintained to the present day and is used several times a year; it hosts the La Touche Cup at the Festival meeting. It is a fascinating course with a wide variety of obstacles but is most well-known for its unique Irish banks from which it inherits its name. The course is a series of bends and more akin to the lay-out of a show-jumping course rather than that of a more conventional racecourse. Interestingly, the lay-out has similarities to the famous Pardubice, which is run each year in the Czech Republic, and more recently to the Cross-Country course at Cheltenham. As a jockey, you run the risk of becoming disorientated; this has certainly happened in the Pardubice, where local riders are known to have some fun by encouraging foreign riders to set the pace and then they hold back to check whether they have taken the correct route – I am not aware that similar tactics have been deployed at Punchestown.

On the Bank course, some of the fences are jumped both ways, including the celebrated Ruby's Double, which is a vast Irish bank with a large ditch on each side. Other obstacles are variously described as a fallen log, a birch roll, a log roll, a French hurdle, a gorse roll and a stone wall along with varieties of banks, including the double, a drop bank and an up bank; for good measure, a few conventional steeplechase fences are included. It remains compulsive viewing and one of the best ways to view the action is to venture out onto the course – most of the race takes place some way from the stands and Punchestown is a large course.

It was in 1992 that I first visited Punchestown and I attended two days of the Festival. While I did not see the running of the La Touche Cup, I did watch the Ladies Perpetual Cup over three miles of the Bank course, which is for amateur riders and – despite the name – bizarrely, it was not just for ladies. The remainder of the racing was highly competitive, with some top-class horses on show. In 1992, the interest from Britain was far less than is the case nowadays as Punchestown racecourse has really blossomed in the last 15 years or so – and has now become very well-known on this side of the Irish Sea. Previously, the interest and mystique of the Festival were enjoyed predominantly by Irish race-goers.

The major rebuilding of the facilities at Punchestown racecourse has been key to its recent success. In 1992, the initial impression was of a prison-block, isolated in the countryside and miles from anywhere. There were high, drab-coloured walls with barbed wire fencing on top and narrow turn-stiles through which to squeeze – being somewhat reminiscent of the old days in trying to access Liverpool's Anfield Football Ground and to stand on the legendary Kop. There were some dated stands at Punchestown, which rose over the top of the walls. From the outside, they did not look welcoming, and, once inside, they were no more than adequate. In time, common sense prevailed and it was agreed to demolish much of the existing visible infrastructure and to make a fresh start.

The finished article is nothing short of sensational and it has made the racecourse into the very best. In fact, little was done to the racecourse itself, which was already acknowledged as being top-class, but the beautifully-designed buildings – housing the facilities required of a modern racecourse with large attendances – cannot be faulted. It is designed like a vast courtyard, with the backs of the large stands having a panoramic view over the sunken paddock. There is terracing around the paddock to accommodate large crowds and to give off the impression of a mini-amphitheatre – with the players being the horses and jockeys preparing for battle out on the racecourse. Furthermore, there are many restaurants and bars. Every conceivable race-goer appears to be provided for, including children and overseas journalists. The stable yard is also a far cry from the tatty old boxes still prevalent at many racecourses.

There is so much space inside the courtyard area that, even at the Festival meeting, it does not feel crowded, a very different scenario from the Cheltenham Festival or indeed most of the other meetings staged there, where it is often a struggle to move around or to secure a decent place in the stands to watch the racing. Hence, I have not rushed to return to the Cheltenham Festival for many years; on this count, Punchestown is far more appealing. It can be argued that the horse racing quality at Punchestown is below that of Cheltenham – a fair point. And British-trained horses do not make a bee-line for Punchestown as much as their Irish counterparts do for Cheltenham – but it is still top-class racing. On race days outside the Festival period, the course may seem quiet as race-goers struggle to fill it. Yet, it is a joy to be able to move around a high-grade racecourse so freely and to have plenty of choices of viewing position.

Punchestown racecourse is one of the largest in Ireland and is similar in size to Leopardstown and Fairyhouse. The steeplechase course is two miles in circumference and the hurdle track runs inside the steeplechase course, after the runners pass the stands; it is about one mile and three-quarters in length. For the most part, the course is flat, except for a hill faced after the horses pass the stands; thereafter, the runners drop down into the back straight. The course must be amongst the fairest around, making it very difficult for a beaten jockey to return and to make excuses about lacking room or securing a fair run; quite simply, there are acres of space around the track, with long straights and big sweeping bends. The beauty of the course is that, despite its size, it is easy to watch the action from the stands. And, if you seek a closer view of the racing, there is, of course, the giant screen, which is nowadays operational at all major race meetings and at many smaller events.

The most spectacular day's racing that I have ever attended was undoubtedly on Thursday, 25 April 2002 at Punchestown. The first race was a two-mile handicap hurdle of special interest to me since I had a share in one of the runners, of whom there were 25. The horse ran on very well at the end to finish a highly creditable sixth, despite running off the minimum weight and being out of the handicap. The second race was the famous La Touche Cup over the Bank course; that year the distance was around four miles. There was heavy media interest in the participation of Sean Connery's Risk of Thunder, who incredibly had won the race for the previous six years, had also finished second in the Pardubice in the Czech Republic – and was now hoping to win the race for the seventh year in succession, despite being a 13-year old and, as usual, carrying nearly 12 stone.

The race was its customary fascinating spectacle. Risk of Thunder was always prominent and jumped impeccably. When they turned in the centre of the course towards the straight, he jumped ahead at the second last and went four lengths clear but was struggling to maintain his lead. As they raced to the last, Risk of Thunder jumped it superbly to steal a length or two and was several lengths clear as they raced towards the line. No doubt, age was beginning to tell and his lead was disappearing with every stride. Somehow, he just held on to win by a neck. There was a hardly a dry eye in the house as he entered the winner's enclosure; he was absolutely exhausted so much so that he was quickly led out to take on oxygen and water. Risk of Thunder returned some 10 minutes later to do a victory lap of the paddock in front of the many adoring fans thronging the rails.

While there were eight competitive races on the card, two others stood out. First, there was a chance to fix eyes on Moscow Flyer, who had just won – in spectacular style – the Arkle Chase at Cheltenham. He did not disappoint in a small field of just six runners; he jumped impressively and went to the front three fences out and came home a very easy seven-length winner giving his regular jockey, Barry Geraghty, an armchair ride. Moscow Flyer was, in time, destined to become one of the greats of National Hunt Racing.

Secondly, there was a chance to watch the irrepressible front runner, Limestone Lad, in the three-mile stayers' hurdle. The horse went off as an odds-on favourite in the nine-horse field and Paul Carberry sent him off into the lead as usual. He won very easily, with the Irish Racing report describing his victory as 'made all, drew clear from four out, unchallenged'. Carberry spent most of the race sitting up high in the stirrups, with occasional glances to see what was happening behind; he, too, enjoyed an armchair ride!

The Punchestown Festival seems to improve every year. The last one that I attended in 2004 was a significant improvement on the 1992 version, with better racing and, of course, much-improved facilities. Even a large fun-fair, set up just across the course behind the winning post in 1992 for the benefit of families, had sensibly been moved to a site outside the track and beyond the winning post: it was barely in the eye-line of serious race-goers.

The real challenge confronting an avid race-goer is how to survive the Festival meeting. If you go for the entire five days, which I have never attempted, I suspect you will need a subsequent holiday to recover. Indeed, my old school mate, Alastair Down, of Channel 4 television fame tells me - from experience - that he is 'done' after about three days. It all depends on how close you stay to the post-racing action since virtually all bars and pubs in Naas, Newbridge, Kildare and Kilcullen have a very busy time during the Festival period: the drinking goes on well into the early hours.

Almost without exception, there is never a poor race meeting at Punchestown. You need a good horse to win a race at the course and the prize money is about the best there is for jump racing in Ireland. For 2023, there were 20 days of racing scheduled with the list dominated by jump racing as the Flat season is limited to just three days. About 10 days of jump racing take place between October and February each year, followed by the five days of the Festival, which is held at the end of April. It may seem late in the season, which carries the risk of unsafe ground conditions, but with Cheltenham, the English and Irish Grand Nationals as well as Easter, the calendar needs to be flexible. In recent years, the organisers have put back the starting times for racing on the first four days of the Festival. The first race is now off in mid-afternoon, which attracts even more race-goers particularly those at work who cannot take an entire day off.

To summarise what Punchestown brings to the party. Its track is superb, the stands, paddock and other facilities are excellent, the racing is exhilarating and the setting is glorious. Undoubtedly, it is Ireland's equivalent of Cheltenham. My one disappointment is the recent decision to build a new track for Flat racing which is currently under construction. I am sure that the most avid fans of Cheltenham would be appalled to see a Flat racing track constructed in its midst since it is all about jump racing. Similar sentiments should apply to Punchestown, famed for its high-class jump racing, which is next to the Flat racing tracks of Naas and The Curragh. Surely, the latter pair should absorb any new capacity required for Flat racing meetings.

Since Punchestown racecourse offers so much, you really should go and experience it for yourself. It is merely a choice of whether you want to experience the course, when there is plenty of space, or to attend the Festival meeting with its large crowds. In reality, you should do both. Then, you will probably want to return to a racecourse over which I have waxed lyrical. I only wish that I lived nearer the course so I could become a full-time member!

21

Roscommon

Rapt attention as they jump the last at Roscommon.

Roscommon, which is located around 100 miles north-west of Dublin, is one of the least-known racecourses in Ireland; partly, this is due to its relative remoteness. Roscommon is also the name of a County and is off the main tourist trail. Nowadays, a quick trip from Dublin via the new motorway network, which branches out from the capital, is very feasible. Roscommon lies in a very peaceful part of the RoI, some 20 miles north-west of Athlone and it is very near to Lough Ree. Roscommon is one of the largest counties but also one of the least-populated and this is in a country not exactly renowned for being over-populated.

In essence, Roscommon is a busy market town, located amid an agricultural area, but it also has a long history, with an impressive castle built in 1269. One of its grisly claims to fame is that it employed a woman as its last public executioner. In 1780, the notorious Lady Betty was found guilty of the murder of her son and sentenced to death. However, she managed to avoid the gallows by accepting a pardon on the basis that she would become the local hang-woman, an office she held for some 30 years.

Horse racing in Roscommon also has a long history dating back to 1837. Aside from a 12-year gap between 1936 and 1948, racing has continued there uninterrupted. At times, bad weather has played havoc with the fixture list and there were several cancellations, due to bad ground conditions, in both 2008 and 2009. Indeed, Roscommon is now basically a summer course with racing between May and September/October: both Flat and jumping meetings are held.

In 2023, nine meetings were scheduled, of which eight were evening meetings. Previously, the fixture list consisted of two meetings, with racing taking place on consecutive days. Such an arrangement seemed sensible for a small course, which is distant from the major cities, and provided a decent boost to the local economy as many race-goers stayed overnight. However, this policy has been superseded so that simple one-day meetings, on either a Monday or a Tuesday, are held: the concentration on evening meetings also raises crowds levels.

The racecourse is straightforward to find, being situated about a mile north-west of the town on the N60 – towards Castlerea – which is a straight, single-carriageway road. Its address – Racecourse Road, Roscommon – is decidedly unimaginative. And, if you use the racecourse website, then it is Racecourse Road, Carrownabricka, Lenabane, Co. Roscommon, which is something of a tongue-twister. The track is generally flat, with an oval shape of about one mile and a quarter. Although it seems a fair test, there is quite a sharp bend after the stands as the runners enter the back straight; furthermore, there is a longer bend coming into the home straight. The minimum distance on the Flat, like many Irish courses without a straight course, is seven furlongs but there are various distances for hurdles and steeplechase races. The average card at Roscommon offers some variety but less so than in the days of mixed meetings.

The track does look distinctly rustic, with the outside railings in the back straight disappearing into brambles and gorse; and there is an old stone wall on the outside as they turn round the paddock bend. The stands are perfectly adequate, with a decent view around the track and across the surrounding countryside. The setting is rural enough, as Roscommon is very much in the countryside, but the surrounding area is less attractive compared with other courses, such as Killarney, Gowran Park, Listowel and Clonmel. The other facilities for race-goers, including the paddock area which is tucked into a corner beyond the stands by the turn into the back straight, are rather cramped; this is quite common with small tracks, where large crowds are generally not anticipated.

The overall ambience at the racecourse gives the impression of it being fairly laid back: its quality of racing is clearly at the lower end. The highlights of the racing calendar at Roscommon are the Connacht National Chase and the Kilbegnet Chase, which is run at the last meeting of the season: it is a Grade 3 race. There is also a listed Flat race earlier in the season. Generally, the prize money at Roscommon is not impressive but it is still quite an improvement on the lower-grade British courses: and the racing normally attracts highly competitive fields. Although top trainers do run horses there on occasions, many races are won by unfashionable trainers and journeymen jockeys.

Roscommon is certainly a friendly course set against a peaceful scene, with the view – on one side – of a sleepy town with its church spires rising above it; to the other side, the views are of fields with large patches of gorse and hills merging into the distance. Very bucolic. Life proceeds at a gentle pace but the evening meetings certainly do attract an enthusiastic crowd and presumably much local interest. It is one of the lower-grade racecourses, set very much in a country meeting environment. There is some indication of greater interest from the big training yards, which should herald an improvement in the quality of the racing.

From personal experience, I am limited in my ability to offer firm views on Roscommon and its racecourse, given that I last attended the racing there in October 1995. The racing was of a poor standard, prize money was modest and there was little atmosphere. However, the meeting was reasonably well-supported, presumably by the locals. With only a small number of meetings held each year, each meeting becomes a significant event for this rather quiet town. That day, the weather was unseasonably good for Ireland. The meeting consisted of eight races and included Flat racing, hurdle races, the Kilbegnet Chase and a concluding bumper. The racecourse's management could not be criticised for a lack of variety.

In November 2022, I did call in at the racecourse and it was very much as I remembered it almost 30 years previously. Very little had changed and the course was effectively de-commissioned during the winter, although the ground looked perfectly fit for racing at the time. Geographically, the north-west and central parts of Ireland have no racing at all between the end of October and April: none of Galway, Ballinrobe, Sligo, Kilbeggan and Roscommon host winter racing.

As an aside, I had to wait at a level-crossing for a train to pass on my way to Roscommon at the near-unpronounceable Knockcroghery – an unusual experience since Ireland, in rural areas, generally missed out on the vast expansion of the railways in Britain from the 1850s onwards. Building railway lines in rural parts of the RoI has tended to be a low priority. I have been to the

RoI on numerous occasions and driven over hundreds of level-crossings but this was the very first time that I had to stop and wait for a train to pass!

Undoubtedly, racecourses, like Roscommon, are the 'bread' and 'butter' of Irish racing. It can only be hoped that they will continue to thrive – the worry is that courses, like Roscommon, are those under the most pressure during an economic slump. Yet, they stand at the heart of horse racing with their long history. At the time of writing, following COVID-19, horse racing in Ireland seems to be reasonably stable. Significantly, the size of fields in Irish racing is materially higher than that in Britain, where many jumping races struggle to have more than a handful of runners.

After all, the upkeep of a racecourse for a maximum of nine meetings a year must be considerable while a short racing season means minimal income for six months or so during the winter, which is hardly helpful for cash flow generation – my apologies for reverting to my previous career as an accountant! It is heart-warming to see how many Irish racecourses – though not all – are well-maintained, often featuring a very wide course to ensure the best possible ground. Realistically, there must be concerns about the very survival of the smaller racecourses, particularly those such as Roscommon, which may have its fixture list ravaged by bad weather during a very wet summer. At a general level, Irish racing does have a good reputation for rescheduling lost meetings – something from which British courses could learn.

Clearly, Roscommon's management has worked hard over the years to keep the racecourse operational – and, indeed, to improve it despite a limited budget. The highlight of these efforts was receiving the 2004 award for 'the most improved racecourse in the country'. The website is not particularly consumer-friendly nor is it clear whether the racecourse has any other associated activities, such as a golf course or corporate hospitality facilities.

Fortunately, it seems unlikely that Roscommon could end up replicating Tralee, which seems destined to become a building site. Hopefully, it can continue providing the entertainment on the racecourse that it has done for so many years. The real worry is that, if racecourses are forced to close – whether a high profile track or a small course with a limited amount of racing – the downhill momentum could be contagious. In that respect, Roscommon could be a soft target. This process took place in England during the 1960s when several racecourses closed, including Manchester, Birmingham and Lewes; more recently, Folkestone and Towcester have shut down. The reasons are varied but finance and housing potential are generally the root causes. Roscommon may not be at the top of the list of racecourses demanding a visit, but it still has much to offer.

22

Sligo

Racing beneath the smart stand at Sligo.

Sligo is William Butler Yeats country. The quintessential Irish poet is revered in these parts, with tourist trails highlighting the spectacular countryside embracing rivers, lakes and forests, which contrast with the rocky headlands and sandy beaches. Yeats is Ireland's most famous poet and Sligo was the place for which he yearned; indeed, his wish to be buried there was granted. His legacy has lived on, with Sligo now renowned as the arts centre of north-west Ireland.

The town has grown quite significantly since I first visited it in 1992. Gone are some of the tatty and derelict buildings of the old town when the port was thriving. In their place, are modern office buildings and an efficient road system, which goes very close to the town centre. A particularly striking feature of the area, that never changes, is the ridge of Ben Bulben, which dwarfs the town. It is a mini-version of the famous Table Mountain, which looks down on Cape Town in South Africa; the ridge is visible all around Sligo, not least from the racecourse.

My venture to Sligo races was way back in April 1992 and started at Galway where I had stayed overnight. The weather was grim, to put it mildly, with April showers of an almost incessant nature: the local roads were soaked. It is some 90 miles from Galway to Sligo, along the N17 with no dual carriage-way, until you join the N4 just south of Sligo. In the swamp-like conditions, it seemed a tedious journey until, some 20 miles south of Sligo, my mother – with whom I was travelling – spotted a pub-sign a mile off the main road. I did not need much encouragement to take a left turn, as – not least – it was just after noon, which seemed a reasonable time of the day for the first pint.

Predictably, the pub was in the middle of nowhere and looked deserted. We plucked up courage and peered inside; there was a semblance of life with a barman talking to a solitary customer. We ordered a beer each but it was not long before the solitary customer, who held two greyhounds on leads, started talking to us. At first, we struggled to guess what he was saying so broad was his Irish brogue. He was certainly very friendly but it soon dawned on us that the pub was effectively his place of business. Initially, he tried to sell us some greyhounds; then he moved on to chickens; then it was horses; then it was donkeys; and then cows, etc. The more we explained that we had no wish to buy any animals and, if we did, we could not take them on a plane, the harder his sales pitch became. If we had taken him up, I think we would have filled up a zoo! It took some time but, finally, we managed to make our exit.

Whenever my mother went racing, car parks were one of her idiosyncrasies. Normally, she left before the last race as she had a total aversion to queuing for the exit. Hence, I had asked our 'friend' about the car parking at Sligo, to which he confirmed there was a large car park as you approached the course. My mother was reassured as we downed the remainder of our pints and drove the 20 or so miles to Sligo racecourse.

Coming from the south, you travel downhill into Sligo; around a half-mile or so before the centre of the town, there is a turning to the right and, within a few hundred yards, the signs of the racecourse are apparent. Horse-boxes were parking at the side of the road and unloading their horses. You could also see the back of the stands and the racecourse entrance at the end of the road. On the right-hand side of the road was a cemetery with the usual outsize memorials, which are so prevalent in Ireland. Just beyond the cemetery was a sign for the car park – the so-called large car park according to our 'friend' at the pub. Frankly, the car park bordered on the bizarre. First, it had a slope leading into it and many large protruding rocks on which you could easily ground a car. Secondly, following the incessant rain, there was more water than grass and, thirdly, the car park was anything but large; it was tiny.

Although I was driving, my mother was quick to voice her disapproval. However, I did manage to beach the car on the largest piece of grass available; it soon became clear that there was no hope of the attendants parking cars in an orderly way. Before we had a chance to get out of the car and brave the elements, another car screeched to a halt near us pursued by a remonstrating attendant. The driver shot out of the car, grabbing a saddle and zip-bag from the back seat, and was then confronted by the attendant suggesting that the car was badly parked and needed to be moved. The driver was the jockey, Tom Taaffe, and he told the attendant in no uncertain terms that his car was not moving. He promptly dashed off and, within an hour, had ridden the first winner of the afternoon.

The first major issue was whether racing would take place at all given the almost incessant rain; we were relieved to find that racing was going ahead. Given that the Irish racing authorities are now more cautious about adverse weather conditions, that might not have been the case today. Back in 1992, racing seemed to take place in Ireland whatever the weather. Those were the days when 'yielding to soft' in Ireland used to equate to a water-logged course in Britain. Heavy ground in Ireland used to resemble ground more typical of the battlefields at the Somme in the First World War. The ground on this day at Sligo was announced as being 'heavy'; in reality, this was a major understatement as the ground was so soft that horses were literally sinking – up to their knees – in it. I cannot recall seeing horse racing take place on ground that was so soft.

The racecourse at Sligo is small – just under a mile in circumference with the home straight being the highest section. The field seems to be permanently on a turn, very much like the famous Roodeye racecourse at Chester. Not surprisingly, visibility is extremely good and the stands are barely necessary; they seem as irrelevant as those at Hexham. The course is dominated by the backdrop of Ben Bulben, which provides a pleasant setting as the racecourse itself is rather austere. The centre of the racecourse seems to be either rough ground or allotments and there is a very unsightly electricity pylon just as the runners turn into the home straight. The paddock is one of the better aspects of the racecourse, which former RoI President, Mary Robinson, graced with her presence in April 1992.

As you might expect, the standard of racing at Sligo is relatively poor – you should not expect to identify any potential classic winners running on the Flat or any serious Cheltenham contenders over the hurdles and fences. But the racing has been competitive and certainly not boring, not least because most days – in the past – provided mixed racing, which is no longer the case. Nowadays, it is either Flat or hurdle races, apart from the rare day over fences. The meeting in April 1992 was a mixed meeting and opened with a three-mile hurdle followed by two Flat races over six and a half furlongs. Two steeplechases followed, before a further Flat race and the inevitable bumper for the finale.

The fourth race on the card, which was a two and half-mile novice chase, will live long in the memory. Given the dreadful ground, the race degenerated into the equine equivalent of a destruction derby on a stock-car track. Twelve runners started; by the time they raced down the hill into the back straight, horse after horse began to throw in the towel. One exhausted horse virtually collapsed into a fence and refused, despite the cajoling of his keen amateur rider. Two more fell, with seven of the remaining nine being either pulled up or just stopping, unable to put in another stride. Only two survivors staggered up the hill into the straight at little more than walking pace; they scrambled over the final obstacle together at which point Minstrel Man managed to find a second gear and came away up the short run-in to win by at least twenty lengths. It was as dramatic a race as I had seen until Red Marauder's heroic Grand National triumph in 2001. Although this race was run over about half the distance of the Grand National, the finishing horses looked even more tired.

There had been indications of problems with the steeplechase track at Sligo – they seemed to recur on this day in April 1992. Furthermore, Sligo staged no racing over fences between 1998 and September 2009. However, the steeplechase track has now been resurrected and it re-opened with three well-supported races offering decent prize money – at least by Sligo standards. Subsequently, steeplechases seem to take place at Sligo just once each year, generally at the September meeting.

For 2023, nine meetings were scheduled and, of these, four were afternoon events, leaving five evening meetings. Six days were allocated to jump racing, including the one day of steeplechasing; the remaining three days were reserved for Flat racing. So, there is variety aplenty. The racecourse website looks impressive with hospitality packages on offer; you sense there is plenty of enthusiasm from the management to provide customers with a good day-out even if the racing quality is at a modest level.

Of course, in terms of quality racing, Sligo is well down the list of Irish racecourses; in reality, it is fairly similar to Roscommon, its nearest neighbour. The former is the most north-westerly course in the RoI and is not renowned for the warmest weather. I suppose that it is hardly surprising that County Donegal, which is further to the north-west and famous for its spectacularly wild weather, lacks a racecourse! Sligo is certainly well worth a visit, assuming that the weather is not too desperate – and you can negotiate the shambolic car parking. Horse racing is held there during the summer months and you need very little imagination to realise why winter racing at Sligo would be a non-starter. The meetings take place from the end of April to October. And, as at Roscommon, the ground-staff have managed to widen the track so that there is always fresh ground available for each meeting.

For a small racecourse, the facilities at Sligo are reasonable. Probably the two best features are the attractive tree-lined paddock and the small circuit, which not only makes viewing easy but also leads to exciting races. Over the years, I have passed by the racecourse and few changes seem to have occurred. Major investment has certainly not reached this north-western outpost of the Irish horse racing community, although the town itself has certainly been more fortunate.

Once you have finished watching the horse racing – assuming you are a golfer – you should not leave Sligo without visiting its two superb golf courses. First, there is the championship course at Rosses Point, with a dramatic green set right out on the point before you head for home; then, a blind tee shot is required to reach the last green, along with the sanctuary of the clubhouse and its commanding views out to sea. Secondly, there is the easier course at Strandhill, which – early in your round – runs alongside a wide, sandy estuary where you can enjoy the sight of horses being exercised. But the golf course still has several tough holes to prevent you from getting too side-tracked.

On a totally different subject, I can highly recommend a visit to Enniscrone on the coast; it is about 30 miles west of Sligo, off the road to Ballina. Apart from hosting another excellent championship golf course, it is the venue of the famous Kilcullen's Seaweed Baths. The building looks quite dated. Once inside, you are allocated a room containing a really deep, old-fashioned bath with steaming water full of sea-weed; there is also an elderly wooden sauna, which is similar to a box. It was explained to me that you should alternate between the bath and the sauna. At the end of your session, (after either 30 minutes or 45 minutes) you should pull the cord above the bath – and then you are drenched with icy water to maximise the effects of the therapy. Whilst – somewhat cowardly – I gave the icy water a miss, I found the bath and sauna very therapeutic and highly refreshing!

23

Thurles

The rather drab paddock and buildings at Thurles.

For some curious reason, my RoI atlas sub-divides the County of Tipperary into North and South Tipperary – it appears to be the only county in the RoI to be split between a north and south. Anyway, Thurles is in North Tipperary and, despite a population of only 8,000, is the second largest town in this part of the county. In fact, Tipperary is one of the most extensive farming areas in a country, where farming is a major industry; it is also famous for its hunting. The most celebrated hunt would seem to be the Scarteen Hunt; it is synonymous with the Ryan family, who have provided many masters over the years. The hunt prides itself on having the best banks and ditches that Ireland can offer: many British hunting enthusiasts travel over for the excitement and are rarely disappointed.

As well as hosting a racecourse, Thurles makes one other major sporting contribution to the RoI. It is the birth-place of the Gaelic Athletic Association

(GAA), which is the organisation responsible for Gaelic Football and Hurling: both sports are passionately followed in the RoI. The second-largest GAA stadium, after Croke Park, is in Thurles and it has a capacity exceeding 50,000, which – for a town with a population of just 8,000 – seems excessive. But it is the home of Munster Hurling, which attracts many spectators from Limerick and its surrounding areas.

Geographically, Thurles, despite being somewhat isolated, is reasonably easy to access. From Dublin, you can use the impressive motorway system by travelling on the M7, past Naas and Kildare, and then proceeding south onto the M8 after Portlaoise: compared with the gruelling slog of by-gone days, the trip is now straightforward. The M8 takes you to within five miles or so of Thurles, with just one right-turn off the motorway for the last few miles. Passing through Thurles' town centre is challenging since several roads converge here; often, it becomes very congested so you need to add at least 20 minutes to your journey time.

If you are travelling from the south, especially from Cork, you should use the M8, until you turn left a few miles from Thurles at the junction near the rather aptly-named village of Horse and Jockey. If you are flying from Britain, a flight to Shannon is normally the best option. However, to reach Thurles, you need to drive – for about 35 miles – along the meandering R503: it is not a good road. But the scenery is pleasant, and it does take you right past the racecourse, which is a mile or so west of the town centre, whose regular congestion you should avoid.

My first visit to Thurles racecourse was on a Sunday in December 1997. I was booked on a day-trip from Heathrow to Shannon: I probably challenged a few driving records by reaching the racecourse within an hour and a quarter of the plane touching down. Just 10 minutes after unbuckling my seat-belt on the plane, I was starting the engine of my hire-car; it took a little over an hour getting out of Shannon onto the distinctly unimpressive R503 and thence to the racecourse. Since my plane did not leave Heathrow until 10am and the first race was at 12.30, it was clear that I should not tarry. In fact, I missed just the first race, while the horse that I part-owned was in the concluding bumper. This express journey is unlikely to be replicated since, these days, hire-cars are now parked elsewhere at Shannon Airport. Back in 1997, my hire-car was conveniently parked about 20 yards from the car-hire desk just outside the arrivals exit.

In February 2001, I again flew to Shannon on a day-trip, although this time I departed from Gatwick. I dutifully checked in at just after 6am for the 7am flight and asked if there was any chance of being allocated a seat with extra leg-room: I am the height of the average second-row forward on a rugby pitch. I received an answer, the like of which I have received neither before nor since, which confirmed that the plane held 175 passengers – and only 25 seats were booked, one of whom was for my brother who was accompanying me; so it appeared I would not be lacking for choice. It was actually quite weird looking around the inside of the plane and trying to spot a passenger amongst the many empty seats! The flight had cost me just £18 return; this was before the days of departure taxes. While the return flight was slightly busier, I had wonderful value for money that day. This scenario is unlikely to recur not only because of higher flight costs and prices but also because Virgin discontinued flying the Gatwick to Shannon route.

Given its long-standing hunting connections, it is hardly surprising that Thurles' racing fixtures are almost entirely jumping meetings: the rare Flat meetings of the past seem to have been superseded. To be sure, there was a Flat meeting in October 2018 – that was the first such event for over a decade! By concentrating on the jumping season, racing at Thurles takes place through the winter months – there were 11 meetings scheduled for 2023. Between the end of March and October, Thurles does not stage racing. Instead, it focuses on winter racing, where abandonments are highly unusual. As a result, indifferent weather is likely, not least it can be very chilly. This problem is best addressed in the town centre which – like most towns in County Tipperary – boasts a wide array of pubs. They are the best places locally to warm up, either with soup or other hot food, before arriving at the racecourse – assuming you are not stuck in traffic!

In common with Sligo, car parking issues also provide some excitement at Thurles. Some race-goers simply abandon their cars on the verge by the road outside the racecourse, while others venture inside, particularly trainers and jockeys, where cars are parked anywhere with sufficient space. The remainder of race-goers approach the fields at the other side of the road, officially marked as car parks. Inevitably, many race-goers struggle to exit the racecourse at the end of racing. As always at RoI racecourse car parks, several tractors are on stand-by to tow out those cars that are well and truly stuck in the mud. I should add that, amongst the cars, there are also horse-boxes and trailers unloading runners – they seem remarkably casual in Ireland about providing separate car parks for horse-boxes and race-goers. On my last visit, I parked in the road and it was certainly more convenient – I recommend that approach.

Thurles hosts good-quality racing, with its fixtures during January and February attracting many Cheltenham Festival hopefuls for their prep races. The quality of racing is similar to that on offer at Ascot during their winter jumping season. The prize money may be less enticing but races at Thurles surely take as much winning as they would at Ascot. Any other similarities between the two racecourses end. The facilities at Thurles must be about the worst you could find at any British or Irish racecourse. Not a place for a nice day-out with your wife or girlfriend, unless they are racing die-hards. And certainly, do not encourage them to dress up!

The racecourse facilities at Thurles were noticeably bad in 1997, the year of my first visit. In the intervening quarter-century – my latest visit was in November 2022 – they have shown little improvement. To be fair, the gents' lavatories, sited under the back of one of the two stands, have acquired stainless steel urinals; previously, you faced a trough. Facilities for bookmakers have also been upgraded. Generally, though, the quality of facilities remains on a par with racing outposts, such as Plumpton or Wye in the late 1960s.

Strangely, the two main stands are sited at an angle to each other. Both have unprepossessing corrugated-iron roofs and, in 2008, were in such a state of disrepair that, in places, you could see daylight through them: the gutters, too, were next to useless when the rain came. One of the stands maintains a partly wooden floor, which I suspect would not pass muster in Britain. While the paddock is a decent size, the amount of grass in its centre erodes on every visit that I make to the racecourse; it is steadily being replaced with a drab-looking wood-chip. Adding to the run-down nature of the paddock area, were two Leylandii trees, which clearly have seen better days; both looked in urgent need of tree surgery to remove their cracked branches, which looked ready to drop off given a strong gust of wind.

Behind a tatty piece of fencing, with various broken slats at one end of the paddock, was a muddy area with a concrete base; this provides a communal shower for horses as they are hosed down before returning to the racecourse stables after racing. I have been to these stables and the word, basic, springs immediately to mind. Furthermore, there were a few small buildings – covered in ivy – near the other end of the paddock, which housed a bar and provided a limited range of food – they looked about as fragile as the pavilion at my local village cricket ground. Again, I am surprised they are able to withstand fierce winds; more generally, it is clear that meeting Health and Safety requirements is not the highest priority on Irish racecourses.

Encouragingly, some minor maintenance work had been undertaken as I noticed on my most recent visit in November 2022. The roofs on the stands have been repaired so that I could no longer see daylight through them. It looked as though some paint had been applied to a few buildings and some – much overdue – tree-surgery had been carried out. Just one large Leylandii remains and it is clearly not in the best of health. And now, there is a large area of tarmac inside the course for owners, trainers and jockeys to park – a significant improvement.

The weigh-room for jockeys is beneath the back of one of the stands and they walk past the bookmakers to access the paddock. The bookmakers seem to have done best from the improvements, as they are installed in a neat square, with a pole at each station, a box attached to connect to a portable computer and a crate on which to stand.

The betting enclosure at Thurles tends to be heaving, even when it is near-freezing – Irish race-goers really do like a punt. I have not encountered much colder weather for racing than I experienced at the Thurles meeting that I attended in January 2001; it was staggering to see the size of the crowd for a mid-week fixture, but such is the popularity of the sport among Irish race-goers. Nevertheless, the crowd looked significantly smaller when I was there in November 2022, which is a worrying sign despite cheaper course admission fees than in England – I paid just €10 for admission, although I have to own up to being a pensioner.

Strangely enough, when I first started to think about writing this book in late 2009, I came across articles in the Racing Post suggesting that the future of the racecourse was in doubt. Apparently, there were plans to build an exotic racecourse complex, with other sports and leisure activities, about four miles away from the site of the existing course. Importantly, Thurles racecourse is family-owned and apparently there have been talks with potential developers of the new complex and discussions about transferring their fixtures to them. Sadly, this would presumably have meant the end of racing at Thurles. Most of these plans were shelved, perhaps because of the poor economic environment at the time. Subsequently, another generation of the Molony family has apparently taken over running the course.

The existing racecourse at Thurles undoubtedly has character and is located in a lovely, rural setting, surrounded by fields on three sides. In the distance is the Devils Bit Mountain, whose image has been turned into the racecourse logo where it sits above two racehorses. The Devils Bit Mountain looks like a mountain, but with a chunk bitten out of its summit. The story is that the Devil, in a fit of temper, took a bite from the mountain and dropped it in Cashel where the famous Rock now stands. Despite the archaic stands, there is good visibility around the course, which seems to be remarkably similar in shape to Gowran Park but is slightly smaller and sharper.

The racecourse is certainly set up for good-quality racing and that is what it gets – with good fields and some class horses in action. The racecourse's excellent drainage is a major benefit – apparently, it has been referred to as Ireland's 'first all-weather course'! The races are extremely competitive with the top trainers being very evident as they run their Cheltenham hopefuls. Despite its excellent drainage, the ground is often testing and horses generally make good use of the communal shower as they return plastered in mud. The jockeys clearly earn their fees and, hopefully, the facilities in the weigh-room are superior to those on offer to the public.

I have been to five meetings over the years, three as a part-owner; each time, we have had a good run for our money even if winning has eluded us. I was also at Thurles in November 2008 when War of Attrition, a subsequent Cheltenham Gold Cup winner, was running at one of the winter mid-week meetings and he was a class winner. I have always been very impressed by the quality of the racing at Thurles. This benefit illustrates what the course has to offer and why it is a very good racecourse, so long as you are not too fussy about stands, bars, lavatories and the like! I think there are two areas where major refurbishment is needed. First, the catering facilities are still inadequate, not helped by an uninspiring website. It waxes lyrical about the quality of their food and offers an extensive hot-food menu, highlighting – 'our bacon and cabbage is a particular favourite with our regular race-goers'! They also supply soup and sandwiches at the back of one of the stands. Even accepting that they race during the winter, the absence of any substantial corporate hospitality facilities still seems unambitious; hence, their hyped-up menu is really directed towards die-hard racing enthusiasts. Secondly, very little seems to be done for winning owners, with no evidence of trophies being presented or the existence of a winners' connections bar where successful owners celebrate with champagne and watch a replay of the race, as is commonplace in Britain.

Despite its shortcomings, I do hope there is no possibility that the racecourse might close because it has a distinctive character, which a new 21st century complex nearby certainly could not replicate. A day at Thurles racecourse, especially in January or February, really is what Irish jumping is all about – not posh stands, but more like the facilities at the average point-to-point but overlaid with quality racing, with the skill and empathy of horse and jockey being very much in keeping with the name of the village just down the road! It is a course that you should visit but dress appropriately, since it can be bitterly cold there!

24

Tipperary

A bucolic environment at Tipperary.

Some 25 miles south-west of Thurles is Tipperary, which is synonymous with the famous First World War marching song – 'It's a long, long way to Tipperary...etc'. Indeed, I recall driving into Tipperary on the N24 from Cahir a few years ago and was greeted by a road-sign which stated, 'Welcome to Tipperary and you have come a long way'. I am also reminded that the town is referred to as 'Tipp' by locals and that it is definitely spelt with two p's!

In fact, this sign was dwarfed by a far larger sign erected to celebrate the Tipperary Sewerage Scheme, which apparently has been funded by the EU. I was pleased to see that some of the vast funds paid into the EU had been put to good use, but I always wonder what the RoI does to secure so much money from the EU – unlike the British Government which seemed incapable of doing so. In addition to all the money going into projects, such as sewerage plants, it seems the RoI has had considerable EU funding for its new motorway system, which suddenly sprung up some 15 years or so ago – this development was particularly welcome as far as I was concerned!

Tipperary is also associated with the legendary, but lucky, winner of the 1928 Grand National at 100-1. As a rank outsider, winning his first-ever race, Tipperary Tim benefitted from a massive pile-up caused by the mighty Easter Hero, who – despite beating 64 other horses, but not the 65th, and carrying a staggering 12 stone, five pounds – narrowly failed to win the 1929 Grand National.

The town centre of Tipperary is full of brightly-coloured buildings, of which many are either pubs or bars. Flag-hanging is popular and, to be fair, does brighten up the town whose outskirts are dominated by drab-looking houses. The busy town centre is congested as the N24 is the main road from Waterford through to Limerick. Add to that, there are sufficient parked vehicles to cause traffic problems, particularly when large lorries try to wind their way through the town's narrow streets. Undoubtedly, the town does have some attractions, but the congestion does not exactly encourage visitors to linger.

During my last visit in November 2022, the town was struggling, in part due to COVID-19. The centre seemed significantly quieter than previously, with fewer pubs and vacant shop-space. Furthermore, there were two very large out-of-town supermarkets – a Tesco and an Aldi – with large car parks; this fact may account for the inactivity in the town centre.

The Tipperary racecourse is on the N24 to the north-western side of the town and within three miles of it. It is located at a place named Limerick Junction, where both railway lines – from Dublin to Cork and Limerick to Waterford – meet. In fact, the racecourse was known as Limerick Junction for many years, rebranding itself as Tipperary shortly before its meeting in May 1986. It is widely believed that many people assumed Limerick Junction was actually in the city of Limerick, which is about 25 miles distant. Over the years, Bangor-on-Dee has had similar problems, with some race-goers and even a few misguided jockeys heading for Bangor on the North Wales coast, which is at least 50 miles away from the racecourse before realising their mistake!

In fact, Limerick Junction railway station does little to impact the local racing scene. Historically, the RoI never participated in the railway-building frenzy which captivated England in the latter part of the nineteenth century. The station bears very little resemblance to the only other 'junction' with which I am familiar – namely, Clapham Junction station which is just outside central London. At Limerick Junction, you will barely notice any trains passing prior to – or during – the afternoon's racing. Few race-goers seem to use the station, unlike the large numbers who alight onto platforms adjacent to, for example, Newbury, Plumpton and Uttoxeter.

Tipperary races has a long history, which is not surprising given its hunting tradition. According to the racecourse website, the first races at Tipperary were held in 1848, with the present course first being used in 1916. It prides itself on being a summer course and the current format has racing starting in April and finishing in October. There were 11 meetings scheduled for 2023, with a three-day meeting in early July. It was a varied programme, including Flat racing and jumping: there were some evening meetings as well.

In common with most Irish racecourses, the simplest way to park is to pull up at the side of the road – as at Thurles – despite it being the main road between Limerick and Waterford. Inside the course, it is not difficult to find your way around. The facilities are perfectly reasonable with two stands and a paddock, which is alongside the racecourse. There is tarmac in abundance and considerable open space, which does not make it particularly welcoming when the wind blows – this was very noticeable when I attended Tipperary races as long ago as October 1996.

It was the last meeting of the season at the racecourse and the word 'bleak' springs instantly to mind. An evening meeting during the summer with fine weather would clearly have made the course much more attractive, especially with the trees in full leaf. It was easy to envisage a decent-sized crowd flocking there from the town and from Limerick, plenty of corporate hospitality, a warm evening and the sun setting in the West.

Unfortunately, the final meeting of October 1996 was very different with grey skies, a cold wind and a modest crowd by Irish standards. The racing was mundane, too, with the first three races being maiden events on the Flat. In fact, the main interest centred on the appearance of Richard Dunwoody, the top English jockey, for a single ride in a hurdle race; there was also a further leg of the Australian/Irish jump jockeys' challenge, which I had encountered at Downpatrick. There were a reasonable number of runners in each race so the racing was competitive, even if the standard was quite low. Overall, there was little to rest in the memory from this day's racing at Tipperary.

The racecourse itself is also rather underwhelming, being a left-handed track of about one and a quarter miles circumference; there is, too, a straight five-furlong course. The racecourse is very flat; the only slight quirk is a very sharp bend after the runners have passed the stands - to ensure they do not go straight on towards the railway station. The straight is quite short, so good views of the runners are very possible. Amongst the English courses, the nearest comparators to Tipperary would be Southwell or Nottingham.

Some years ago, the straight five-furlong course attracted interest from British horses; there were some high-value races. Sadly, this interest seems to have waned of late. The racecourse has suffered badly from water-logging at times, even despite the lack of winter racing. Somewhat ironically, the racecourse's website used to boast of its watering system! Few Irish racecourses have much need of this equipment, although the ground at Tipperary can dry up very quickly when the sun shines and there is a brisk wind.

In all honesty, Tipperary racecourse is not high on my list to revisit – there is comparatively little of note to see. The track is distinctly uninteresting and the facilities were no more than adequate; perhaps, a visit in mid-summer might reshape my views. Neither is the location very attractive, despite the rural location – it seemed bleak in the cold and grey weather. Of course, race-goers in Ireland are spoilt with stunning locations at such tracks as Killarney, Punchestown and Listowel, not forgetting the one-off sea backdrop at Laytown. At Thurles, where the facilities are also basic, the quality of the racing and the overall atmosphere compensates for these shortcomings: the same cannot said for Tipperary.

Tipperary lacks well-known races and few decent horses are attracted there. But due to the high number of runners, racing is generally competitive. In recent years, the prize money on offer has risen appreciably, thereby providing a better quality of racing. Importantly, the racecourse has been successful in attracting crowds during the summer months: its restaurant in the refurbished facilities on the first floor of the Limerick stand has become very popular.

The plans to build an all-weather track, as part of an €18 million redevelopment project at the course, remain live. Seemingly, the Irish Racing authorities are determined to install a further all-weather track after Dundalk: Tipperary has been selected as the preferred location. According to the Racing Post in October 2022, the plans have stalled because an appeal has been launched by two local residents against planning permission being granted. Prior to this intervention, construction work had been due to start in late 2023. On this basis, the new track would have opened at the end of 2024 and there would have been no racing at Tipperary during the construction work.

Assuming the redevelopment project proceeds, Tipperary racecourse will look quite different: the whole operation will be much larger, with the Dundalk investment providing the template. It appears that the famous straight five-furlong sprint course will be removed – a regrettable aspect of the planned redevelopment. An increase in fixtures per year – up by as much as 30 – has been proposed, which would boost employment opportunities for local people.

Hopefully, all goes according to plan – and provides Tipperary racecourse with a long-term future, as well as boosting its profile. Nevertheless, my somewhat negative views on the racecourse abide. And, given my antipathy to all-weather horse racing, I fear that Tipperary racecourse may eventually look very similar to the all-weather racing at Southwell!

25

Tralee

Racing at Tralee during its halcyon days.

Writing this chapter may well prove to be a fruitless exercise as it is now becoming increasingly apparent that horse racing at Tralee has finished. But, as a course with a colourful history going back over a century, it feels wrong to disregard it. Rumours had persisted for several years that its days were numbered, with property speculators waiting to pounce and to convert the racecourse into a housing estate. In 2008, Tralee joined Mullingar, Baldoyle, Tuam and Phoenix Park in closing, thereby, becoming the fifth course to shut down in the RoI since the 1960s.

Over the years, there have been reports in the racing press of lengthy negotiations between the racecourse's directors and potential developers. There was always the hope that the racecourse might be saved, but this seemed to have been extinguished: the final meeting was held there in 2008. Originally, the farewell event was the Rose of Tralee Festival meeting at the end of August. Uncertainty over the racecourse's future and heavy rain during the summer of 2008 resulted in just one day's racing taking place. However, two lost days were re-instated so that Tralee's farewell races were held on 30 September and on 1 October 2008. After that, it was all over for Tralee race-goers. Ironically, the racecourse sale was concluded at the wrong time for the developers since demand for property was falling due to the financial crisis in 2008/09 and the subsequent recession.

Tralee is located in the centre of County Kerry. As a town, it boasts a very attractive centre although the urban sprawl – and the drab properties – on its outskirts are far less easy on the eye. Hopefully, the new homes to be built on the racecourse will be rather more interesting and colourful. The town is in a lovely part of Ireland, near the coast and some 15 miles from Killarney; it offers glorious scenery, along with a spectacular links golf course.

Tralee was one of the three racecourses in the County, along with Killarney and Listowel. All three racecourses were famous for their festival meetings. Killarney set the ball rolling in July with a three or four-day fixture. Then Tralee took centre stage towards the end of August with a six-day meeting before Listowel upstaged them both with its seven-day Festival towards the end of September.

There is a long history of racing in Tralee, which regrettably appears to have drawn to a close. Research shows that the first recorded meeting took place in 1767 and lasted for seven days. This seems an inordinately long time for a race meeting in those days – perhaps it was also an excuse for a big party. It reminds me of the story about the visitor to County Kerry, who was in a pub one sunny evening in May. He enquired of the landlord when the pub closed – the reply was September!

In fact, racing was staged at various locations around Tralee over the years before the racecourse at Ballybeggan Park became its permanent home: racing started there in 1889. Its overriding feature has been a high limestone wall, which encircled the course so that it was barely visible from the outside. Originally, it was a deer park and the wall was built from stone quarried from the centre of the racecourse. The racecourse looked quite quaint and appealing – and had good visibility. The main downside was that it backed onto an industrial estate at the bottom end of the track.

To the naked eye, the racecourse looked almost square. In fact, it was just over nine furlongs in circumference, so the maximum length of any side could only have been three furlongs at most. The track was on a slight slope with the finishing straight being uphill. The stands were substantial and there was ample space around the enclosures, with a large paddock on a well-mown lawn enclosed by a smartly clipped hedge: it was at its best for the Festival in August. In short, the racecourse offered many positives. It seems a crying shame for it to be turned into a building-site – there must be many more suitable candidates for this fate and I can certainly think of some suitable names on this side of the Irish Sea!

I went to the races at Tralee on 4 June 2001, which was a Bank Holiday Monday in the RoI. I had a vested interest in a horse, which was due to run in the concluding bumper. It was unusually good weather for a Bank Holiday – and for Ireland – and this drew a large crowd. Unlike my mother, I am normally relaxed about car parking, but it was a struggle as the cars were parked bumper-to-bumper – she would not have been impressed. Luckily, I was in no great hurry to leave.

For me, more of a concern was the dry weather since it was evident that the track had not been watered. I assume that Tralee lacked the wherewithal to do so, as it is so rarely needed in Ireland. The lack of water did, though, play havoc with the racing. There was a long list of withdrawals on account of the ground, which had firmed up. Our trainer, Michael Hourigan, confirmed that his son, who had ridden in an earlier race, described the ground as 'hard and rough' - it was a simple decision for our horse to be withdrawn.

Nevertheless, having travelled some distance, it was disappointing not to have a runner but it did not detract unduly from an enjoyable afternoon's racing. There were six hurdle races as well as the bumper and it was challenging to pick the winners. As the day wore on, it continued to get warmer and warmer, not something that is typical at an Irish racecourse. Unquestionably, the backdrop of the mountains behind the course in the bright sunshine looked magnificent.

The racing that day was obviously of a far lower quality than that on offer at the famous Rose of Tralee Festival, which had always taken place in August. That race meeting was an integral part of the International Rose of Tralee Festival when the town is heaving with visitors. Prior to the autumn of 2008, the Festival had staged valuable races, attracting very competitive fields, with a rich variety of events ranging from Flat racing to hurdles and steeplechases. For most punters, winners proved elusive. Moreover, there was the added glamour of well-dressed ladies competing for the Rose of Tralee prize.

Where did it all go so wrong that a popular track should have to close down? Was it the fact that there were just two events each year, namely a two-day meeting in early June and the six-day Festival in August? Sadly, it seems winter racing there was a non-starter and that such a small amount of racing could presumably no longer justify its existence and cover its costs. Instead, property developers dangled a carrot, which was just too good to turn down. It is a great shame and

Irish Racing is inevitably the poorer without such a unique track as Tralee: its hugely popular August Festival fixture has now been taken over by Killarney.

Is there any hope that the racecourse will be returned to racing? I visited the track in September 2010 and there were no signs of any building work underway – and this was almost two years since the farewell meeting was held. The stands and paddock were still apparently untouched and the track was still visible, even if it lacked rails. Apart from a small allotment being installed on part of the track, just past the stands, there were few other obvious impediments – financial issues aside – to re-opening the racecourse. Given the vast number of houses for sale in the RoI, following the credit crunch and subsequent recession, the demand for new homes will surely have abated.

In the intervening years, the racecourse has been used for point-to-points. But on my last visit in October 2022, the entrance was boarded up and there were warnings of guard dogs being at large inside. A faded Guinness banner remained on the wall outside, which presumably dates back to the farewell meeting in 2008. It was not clear what the guard dogs were actually protecting, because the stands were in a state of disrepair. It may be a Health and Safety-driven initiative to ensure nobody gets inside, sustains an injury and then sues the current racecourse owners.

Interestingly – until recently – if you had accessed the Irish Racing website and selected racecourses, you were provided with the names of 27 racecourses, including Tralee: it merely stated that there were no fixtures. It is now 15 years since the last race meeting at Tralee; it is very unsatisfactory that the site is neither a racecourse nor an active building site. Of course, life often moves slowly in Ireland; after all, it took many years for building work to start on the old Limerick racecourse. Hopefully, an entrepreneur or consortium could secure ownership of the racecourse, before any building work starts, and resurrect horse racing there. A forlorn hope, but the racecourse has real potential and it would surely be a real boost to the town and to local tourism. The location of the course is now very close to the Tralee by-pass, which would facilitate access on race days – rather than driving through the town as in the past. So, here's hoping!

26

Tramore

Tackling the tight bends at Tramore.

Tramore is a small, traditional seaside town, a few miles away from the bustling city of Waterford, on the south coast of Ireland. It has a long sandy beach and plenty of seaside accommodation. But, like many English seaside towns, it all looks rather dated, as many holiday-makers now prefer to fly abroad to warmer climates. Maybe the recession and the COVID-19 pandemic will restore the popularity of seaside holidays, both in the UK and in the RoI, thus obviating the need to fly and face the laborious task of trudging through airport security, notwithstanding all the other delays that are so frequently encountered nowadays at airports.

Driving into Tramore, you are confronted by the out-sized sign announcing that the new sewerage scheme was generously provided by the EU, in a similar vein to the new sewerage facilities provided in Tipperary. I still fail to understand why such schemes are so plentiful in the RoI, whereas in Britain – even prior to Brexit – few were seen. Otherwise, there is plenty of new housing and new roads. It can be assumed that Tramore is a popular commuting town for workers in Waterford, one of the biggest cities in the country.

The connection with Waterford is not lost on the racecourse, which was formerly known as Waterford and Tramore. In recent years, its name has been increasingly abbreviated to Tramore. Even so, there is still a high wall on the racecourse, opposite the stands on the far side of the back straight, which has Waterford and Tramore painted in big letters, thereby making it clear to race-goers where they are. I question the rationale for renaming a racecourse. While simply rebranding the racecourse as Tramore is factually correct – in common with Edinburgh being renamed as Musselburgh – Mallow's superseding by Cork seems unjustifiable.

Tramore racecourse sits on a hill about half a mile inland; the stands face to the north so there is virtually no sea view – a shame since a sea view would be spectacular: unquestionably, such a view makes Brighton racecourse far more attractive. Instead, the north-facing outlook at Tramore and the high wall on the far side of the course – where there is a housing estate with some smart properties – mean the view is rather different. Indeed, the sea view only materialises when you reach the car park, which is in a field on the other side of the road behind the stands; conveniently, only a short walk is needed to access the racecourse. To appreciate fully the stunning view, you need to stand beyond the two fences just past the stands, from which – it appears – the public are banned.

Racing has a long history in Tramore as the course website confirms. Racing began there as long ago as 1785 on the strand; it continued right up until 1911, when sadly the strand course was apparently lost to 'the ravages of the sea'. The website reassures race-goers that the racecourse is now in a safer place. Certainly, up on Graun Hill, this is self-evident, with no likelihood of the sea flooding it! Even so, Tramore has suffered water-logging problems, which has played havoc with its four-day August Festival meeting, most notably in 2012 when the meeting was completed but only after postponements.

Tramore racecourse has had its facilities upgraded over recent years as reported on its website. They are certainly more than adequate but they are rather cramped; after all, Tramore is a small venue and you cannot reasonably expect the space that exists at such racecourses as The Curragh, Leopardstown and Punchestown. In essence, everything at Tramore is small, including the race track itself. Its best feature is probably the attractive paddock which is home to some palm trees.

The track is clearly the smallest in Britain and Ireland. The circuit at Fakenham is just under a mile; Chester, Fontwell Park and Newton Abbot are just about a mile per circuit; but Tramore is barely seven furlongs. The other problem facing the runners is the camber of the track – it is far from flat. In the short home straight, the track is uphill, then there is a sharp turn to the right, followed by another sharp turn, before a downhill run in the back straight; next is a long turn, still going downhill, before turning uphill once again into the home straight. On the steeplechase track, there are two fences in the home straight, another two in the very short uphill section and just one fence in the back straight; then, there is a longish run to the home straight. For hurdle races, there are two hurdles in the home straight, with a third in the short uphill section after the home straight, and a fourth in the back straight.

Describing parts of Tramore's racecourse as 'straight' is somewhat of a misnomer. In fact, only part of the back straight merits that description. Subsequently, the runners are faced with going downhill – at some speed – before having to negotiate the long bend into the home straight. With such a sharp track, the Flat races are run over comparatively long distances; indeed, the shortest distance appears to be one mile and four furlongs: there is no chance of a five-furlong or six-furlong sprint. A race of over one mile and four furlongs requires almost two laps of Tramore's track. For races of over two miles and six furlongs, which seem to be a standard distance at the track, the runners pass the winning post no less than four times. In doing so, they jump 17 fences, which seems plenty bearing in mind that the Ulster National at Downpatrick is three miles and four furlongs in length with 16 fences.

I am providing this insight to highlight the somewhat hair-raising nature of this track, particularly in jump races. For me, it evokes memories of that old country track at Wye in Kent, which closed in the 1970s. It was reported that several jockeys welcomed the news of its closure and remarked that they would sleep easier at night in the knowledge that there was no more racing at Wye. Undoubtedly, it was a tight track with a downhill back straight and the circuit was barely a mile in length. The races at Wye always seemed to be run at breakneck speed, which led to some spectacular spills and not just at the obstacles.

Whilst a track with a bad reputation may be problematic for jockeys, it often leads to some great entertainment for the spectators so long, of course, that it does not hold any additional danger for the horses. Tramore has certainly had its fair share of dramas, with horses slipping up from time to time on the sharp bends; this is a particular problem if the ground dries out and then there is a shower. There is also the less well-publicised issue of jockeys remembering how many laps of the track they have completed – there have been embarrassing incidents of miscounting in the past.

More specifically, this issue came to the fore in the Newtown Handicap Steeplechase run over two miles, five furlongs and fifty yards at Tramore on 31 December 2007. There were 14 runners and the distance meant that just over three laps of the track had to be covered. Unbelievably, every single jockey rode a finish on the penultimate lap, so much so that nine of the runners were pulled up while the other five jockeys managed to rally their mounts: the favourite, Mr Aussie, eventually prevailed. All the jockeys were hauled in front of the stewards and widespread suspensions followed. They might have been more generously treated if it had been the New Year's Day fixture a day later. Clearly, the stewards were in no mood to be lenient.

Tramore's reputation as a challenging track almost came to an end when its scheduled closure was announced; it was to be replaced by a new racecourse. In December 2006, according to the racecourse website, Waterford County Council granted permission for a new racecourse to be built at nearby Lisselan. It was confirmed, too, that work had already commenced on the construction of the track, which would comprise a one-mile four-furlong left-handed circuit with a width of 80 yards – something very different from the current set-up at Tramore. The plan was that the new racecourse would boast impressive stands, which could accommodate up to 10,000 spectators. However, this major project seems to have come to a halt, presumably on financial grounds. Over 16 years later, racing continues at Graun Hill. Interestingly, in recent years, the facilities have benefited from various upgrades. Moreover, further work seemed to be ongoing when I last visited the course in November 2022.

Whatever happens, there will be many disappointed race-goers if the existing track is closed down – even if, as a result, some jockeys will sleep better! Being so unique, the course certainly has loads of character, while its contours do lead to some exciting racing as I discovered when I attended one of the four days of the Festival Meeting held every August. While it was as long ago as 1998, the memory of entertaining racing on a fine, if somewhat chilly, summer's evening, abides. There was a sizeable crowd packed into the enclosures and a decent variety of racing, with races on the Flat, over hurdles and fences – and some close finishes. On the other hand – and much more recently – there was the amazing performance of Willie Mullins' horse, Gaelic Warrior, who won a two-mile maiden hurdle in December 2022 by a staggering 86 lengths. The odds of 1/12 were hardly attractive. With 10 runners in the race, it seem astonishing that the starting price could be so short, given the potential hazards of the hurdles track; indeed, one of the runners did slip up on a bend.

In recent years, Tramore has increased the amount of its racing, with 12 days being scheduled for 2023. Racing takes place over most of the year, with the main meeting being the four-day Festival in August; there is also a highly popular meeting on New Year's Eve and on New Year's Day for those who are still standing after the festivities of the night before. The meetings are focussed on jump races, which presumably recognises the racecourse's inadequacies for staging Flat racing. In short, Tramore is a distinctly quirky course and is well worth a visit. You are unlikely to encounter a boring day's racing there since the racing is well-supported. Furthermore, the runners are easy to see since they are never very far from the stands: all of the obstacles are nearby as well.

The August Festival is probably the prime time to attend racing at Tramore. The weather should be good and the view from the course over the sea – at least from the car park – is spectacular. Visiting Tramore during the winter can be miserable, if there is significant wind, since the racecourse sits on top of a hill and is therefore very exposed. My visit in November 2022 saw me at the course at 8.30am when there were near hurricane-force winds and driving rain. You could barely pick out the sea due to the thick spray coming horizontally off the water. The only benefit for me was that I had taken the ferry from Fishguard to Rosslare on the previous day, so I was very grateful to be on land, rather than at sea, in conditions like that.

27

Wexford

Jumping the second last at Wexford against a marine background.

The final leg of my odyssey around Ireland's racecourses takes me from Tramore to Wexford, which is in the south-east corner of Ireland and is therefore a short journey since Tramore is Wexford's nearest racecourse neighbour. Indeed, Wexford is nearer to some UK racecourses than to some of its Irish counterparts. After all, the ferry from Rosslare to Fishguard, combined with a short drive across the western part of Wales, will take you to Ffos Las, which must be considerably nearer than Sligo and Ballinrobe in Ireland's north-west.

The course is easy to find as it is situated on the road into Wexford assuming you approach the town from the west on the N25. It is on the outskirts of the town and therefore is not in a rural setting, unlike many Irish racecourses. Fortunately, there is ample car parking and the course opens up once you are inside: it cannot be described as cramped. The backdrop from ground level, though, is hardly stunning as the racecourse backs onto housing estates – similarly to Tramore – and, therefore, it is rather low on the list of my most attractive courses. Furthermore, you are very conscious of the town and houses around you; it is very similar to the old racecourse at Limerick.

Over the years, there have been some worrying reports about the track and it seemed that some trainers were reluctant to race their horses at Wexford. In common with Tramore, the track had a reputation for being tight and badly banked. Clearly, it is a sharp track, with the ground often drying up quickly to give firm conditions – it only needs a shower to make the track difficult and, at times, potentially dangerous.

In July 2003, I visited Wexford races for an evening meeting – with lovely weather. However, the ground had dried out and the going was officially 'firm'. The opening race was the first division of the mares' maiden hurdle with 12 runners. Tragically, two of the horses were killed; one of those fatal falls involved the promising jockey, Kieran Kelly, who was promptly stood down for the rest of the meeting. Even more desperate was the tragic news that, four weeks later to the very day, Kieran Kelly suffered another terrible fall at Kilbeggan and paid the ultimate penalty.

When I heard this appalling news, my mind immediately switched back to that evening at Wexford and whether the fall there was a contributory factor to subsequent events at Kilbeggan. Jump jockeys are amongst the bravest sportsmen around and make light of serious injuries, since they need to earn a living. Many cannot afford to be on the sidelines, and they are well-known for concealing the extent of their injuries, especially if they are concussion-related. Sadly, some injuries are not obvious, and sometimes it is only a subsequent fall which highlights the extent of previous damage.

That evening's opening race left a bitter taste in the mouth; thankfully, the remaining races were run without any similar incidents. It is also quite difficult not to enjoy an evening race meeting in the sun, even if the quality of the racing is moderate – the card consisted of five hurdle races followed by two bumper races. This scenario was not unusual at Wexford. Being stuck out on a limb geographically and with poor reports about the track, it was largely ignored by the top stables so that the quality of its racing remained at the lower end.

When I visited the course, it was right-handed with a short straight and was almost triangular in shape: Kempton Park, probably, is its nearest British equivalent. However, some quite radical changes have been introduced over the last 15 years or so. Initially, the circuit was enlarged by about two furlongs so that now it is nearer one mile and four furlongs in circumference. This change brought major improvements, with less sharp bends – and it has alleviated many of the safety issues discussed above.

The next change was decidedly radical – and something I had not encountered previously. Wexford's management resolved to switch the course from being right-handed to being left-handed; this policy was implemented in April 2015. By all accounts, trainers and jockeys appear to have welcomed this change. It was less enthusiastically received by the paying public since the winning post moved to the other end of the home straight – not surprisingly, the stands did not. Now, the stands are positioned by the last two fences, whilst the winning post is some 400 yards away, planted in front of the car park. With neither the bookmakers nor the punters near the photo-finish, betting income from photo-finishes will presumably have fallen appreciably.

For years, horse racing crowds have generally preferred to congregate near the finish so it unfortunate that this option is no longer feasible at Wexford. If you visit the beautiful racecourse of Chantilly – to the north of Paris – in France, you will see something similar with sprint races on their straight course: the winning post is sited about 400 yards past the stands. This set-up leads to the somewhat anomalous situation whereby, after about three furlongs of a five-furlong race, the horses pass the stands: they gallop into the distance where the business end of the race is decided. At Wexford, it is now very difficult to see from the stands which horse is ahead at the winning post – or indeed to see when the runners are passing it. The drainage contractor from Wexford, with whom I chatted when he was working at Kilbeggan, was certainly not a fan of this radical change due principally to the winning post issue: he is far from alone in holding this view.

In the past, the racecourse used to stage all forms of racing with Flat, hurdle and steeplechase events; there seemed to be no obvious preference other than trying to provide a variety of entertainment for the summer holiday crowds. However, the third change made by the management in 2016 was to abolish Flat racing at Wexford, seemingly sparked by a ruling that maximum fields of only 10 runners were permissible following the change of direction of the track. It seems jumping is the winner from the switch and Flat racing has been the loser.

The facilities at Wexford are certainly functional rather than being palatial. In truth, few Irish racecourses have really smart facilities, probably only the likes of The Curragh, Leopardstown, Galway, Punchestown and Fairyhouse. After all, Wexford is just a small racecourse and its infrastructure reflects that status. Nevertheless, Wexford has much nicer facilities than Thurles but that is not the highest of compliments. The former's paddock is probably its best feature, with pretty flowers adding some colour to the overall spectacle.

Having opened as recently as 1951, Wexford racecourse is one of the newest in Ireland; over the years, it has had its ups and downs and particularly just over a decade ago. At the end of the 2010 season, serious concerns about the state of the course were raised – and meetings were cancelled. This issue looked to have been resolved when the meeting on 15 April 2011 attracted an astonishing 431 entries – with 102 horses entered for the opening maiden hurdle alone. Unfortunately, during the evening meeting at the end of July 2012, there was a major pile-up as the runners entered the straight in a Flat race: six of the 14 runners failed to finish. This type of headline certainly cannot help a racecourse, but – in horse racing – such accidents do happen. It is probable that these events were a catalyst for some of the changes implemented subsequently.

Wexford's tenacity in overcoming its challenges is admirable. The racecourse could so easily have closed down, due to lack of interest. However, strong support locally and considerable hard work behind the scenes, in particular by Michael Murphy, who was the course manager from 1989 to 2021, ensured its survival. His name has always been prominent on the racecourse website and it is clear that the racecourse needed a major boost in the 1990s to persuade the racing fraternity to support it.

Since I was there in 2003, the course has undergone the radical changes described above. Moreover, the track is now much friendlier to horses and jockeys, with better cambering on the bends. Surely, any adverse comments a generation ago about the track being dangerous should be consigned to history. No longer is it sidestepped by the leading trainers and better races are now being run at the track. Indeed, the 2022 Grand National winner, Noble Yeats, won his opening race of the 2022/23 season at Wexford – it was a listed race over two miles and seven furlongs.

Now that the racecourse is clearly becoming more popular with owners, trainers and jockeys, better crowds should be expected. In time, better-class races will be staged and sponsorship should be boosted. I should add that the Wexford Racecourse Supporters Club has played a key role in ensuring the survival of the racecourse, especially during the many lean years.

In fact, despite Flat racing being abolished, the course still maintains an 11-day fixture list. The 2023 calendar showed 11 meetings, starting in early March and finishing at the end of October. Five of these events were afternoon meetings and there was racing on two consecutive days in both June and October. The course is clearly at its best during meetings on summer evenings. I know, too, from my own experience that Wexford's meetings are very popular with the local community as well as attracting many tourists. Despite the course now being limited to jump racing – assuming that winter racing there has been ruled out due to wet ground concerns – Wexford does offer a nice climate in the south-east of the country. Moreover, it is located by the sea so you would definitely be warmer there than at Thurles on a chilly January afternoon!

While Wexford is certainly worth a visit, it is not one of the most attractive Irish courses. The racecourse lies on the edge of town; in this respect, it has similarities to Newton Abbot in Devon. Undoubtedly, the racecourse is improving and I am so impressed by the management's resolve to ensure the course's continued survival: the quality of the racing there is also rising. The future looks distinctly promising: the website is very positive about the experience of a day at Wexford races, as well as being informative. In hyperbolic style, it describes the racecourse as being 'one of the finest tracks in Ireland', a claim that is dubious, to say the least. In the past, Wexford had a countdown on its website of the number of days remaining to its next meeting but this seems to have been abandoned – they clearly welcome change there. It will certainly be interesting to assess where the next 'left-field' initiative could materialise. And it might tempt me to pay another visit to the racecourse!

Epilogue

C'est magnifique – the spectacular course at Auteuil with the Eiffel Tower behind.

My trip around Ireland, though taking a number of years, has been both fascinating and enjoyable. Hopefully, I have convinced most of you, if not all, that Irish racecourses merit a visit; perhaps for a few of them, one visit may suffice! Regrettably for me at least, Dundalk comes bottom of the pile – not because I am against Dundalk but because of a strong aversion to all-weather racing, which seems so colourless and boring. I accept that it does serve some purpose in providing racing when bad weather persists. I still cannot reconcile going to a stadium for horse racing! Tipperary is likely to be second-bottom – assuming that its all-weather track goes ahead. I sincerely hope they do not convert it into a stadium as well!

My one major concern, as I complete this book in 2023, is the state of the Irish economy, as it recovers, like other countries, from the ravages of the COVID-19 pandemic. So far, the signs seem positive – despite falling attendances at some race meetings. The 2024 fixture list is very similar to its 2023 predecessor. Hopefully, the current level of racing can be maintained. It is noticeable, though, that the number of runners in Irish racing has diminished over the years, but they still seem to be higher than in Britain. No longer do the bumper races attract the maximum number of runners as often as they did previously. Nor are 30-runner fields in maiden hurdles at Naas and Navan so common. Some analysis suggests that the number of horses in training has declined – not something that is the case for either Willie Mullins or Gordon Elliott, whose stables now house a vast number of horses compared with leading Irish trainers in the past; sadly, too, many smaller trainers have handed in their licences.

One of the joys of going to Ireland is meeting the Irish people. While I am sure their indomitable spirit and friendliness will endure, they have faced many challenges in the past: their resilience is such that they generally seem unflustered and laid-back. Even during the financial crisis over a decade ago, there seemed to be little violent complaint from the Irish people, unlike in Spain and Greece where frequent demonstrations and riots took place. It was apparent, though, that many young people had decided to live elsewhere: some emigrated to North America or to Australia in the hope of finding lasting employment. In time, many may well return as the Irish economy recovers from COVID-19 and the recent downturn.

During my visits just over a decade ago, it was noticeable that prices were being cut in a drive to secure business. Rates for accommodation and leisure activities had been slashed, along with the real necessities of life - such as a pint of beer in a pub. Interestingly, in 2013, the price of racecourse admission at Punchestown was advertised at €18 per day for the Festival in April but just €10 for all other days. Such figures compared with £15 or so at many ordinary racecourses, such as Plumpton and Fontwell Park: and, outside its March Festival, Cheltenham charged somewhat more. My last visit to Ireland in 2022, following the end of COVID-19, suggests some prices have risen, especially in the case of hotel accommodation. But entry fees to racecourses in Ireland remain quite modest: in November 2022, I paid, as a pensioner, just €10 to be admitted into Thurles; the adult rate generally was €15.

In the past, Irish people have confronted many crises. It is to be hoped that Irish racing can continue to flourish and provide the enjoyment that its people cherish and overseas visitors seek. It would be desperately disappointing if other racecourses follow the apparent lead of Tralee and exited the scene. So do not miss the opportunity of a visit. I suggest you head first to Punchestown and, if you want a smaller track offering real charm, then you should try Downpatrick in NI.

Based on my trip to the Ballymácad Hunt meeting at Oldcastle on 29 April 2012, attending a point–to-point in Ireland is also quite an experience. Such an event really is country sport at its best. The course is built around various fields, with open gates to allow the runners through. Despite the time of year, it was a bitterly cold day, with a fierce wind blowing across the hillside below which the course was laid out. The jockeys changed in what resembled a pair of 38-ton lorries, neatly parked at right angles, with their tarpaulin-covered sides strapped down: the scales were at one end. The racing was serious enough. Indeed, it is at such meetings that some top steeplechasers start their careers: winners of just a single Irish point-to-point can often fetch high prices at the special sales that are now being held, particularly the event at Cheltenham each April. Not surprisingly, the facilities at Oldcastle were both sparse and spartan – to say the least. The bitter wind ended my visit prematurely before I could last out the eight-race card – I am sure it is warmer in Britain in January than it was on that day at Oldcastle!

For jump racing fans wishing to go further afield, you should put Auteuil in Paris at the top of your list. The racing is spectacular, over a very varied collection of obstacles, some of which can be jumped from different sides in the same race. The core track is a figure-of-eight but it has various additions, so the lay-out is complex to put it mildly! It is also very cheap to enter a French racecourse; but, since they are often poorly attended, there is not much of an atmosphere. I went to Pau in the south of France and it was 'entrée gratuite', which means free entry. Saint-Cloud in Paris puts on top-class Flat racing: the entry fee during the week is often €5, or just €3 for pensioners. Over the years, I have visited various French racecourses and the lay-out of the tracks, like Auteuil, is often difficult to fathom. Every steeplechase race, especially if it is a cross-country event, takes place on a course more akin to a show-jumping event at Hickstead; there are twists and turns galore so it is hardly surprising that jockeys take the wrong course quite regularly. I have yet to visit Le Lion d'Angers, which stages a cross-country race over 50 or so obstacles: it is believed to be the longest race in Europe.

For the real jumping enthusiast, a visit to the Pardubice in the Czech Republic is a must. The race takes place each year on the second Sunday of October. The racecourse contains all manner of obstacles, including the famous – and very formidable – Taxis, which is right in front of the stands; there are also ploughed fields, which form part of the course. In total, there are 60 fences on the racecourse, which are used for various races. At one point, there is a row of eight steeplechase fences alongside one other – I have no idea how a jockey knows which one of the eight he is supposed to be jumping. Perhaps this explains why local jockeys often have fun by letting foreign jockeys take up the running and watching them get lost!

For something slightly different, you can try Waregem in Belgium for the Great

Flanders Steeplechase, which takes place each year on the Tuesday after the last Sunday in August. The course is tight, with all kinds of jumps – the racing is interspersed with the occasional trotting race. The most unusual aspect about this venue is that the starting time for each race seems to be vague – races are run when everybody is ready rather than at a specified time.

While, as a rule, Irish people are laid back, their horse racing activities are very efficiently organised; they ensure that races nearly always start – the notorious delay some decades ago in starting the Ulster Derby at Down Royal due to loose sheep on the course was a rare exception – at the precise time allotted. They love the sport. Let us hope that horse racing in Ireland can continue to prosper so that you can enjoy their generous hospitality and experience what their racecourses have to offer – as I have done. Of course, the economic climate remains a concern. But now is a good time to visit some of the stunning courses that I have done over the years. So, as they say in Ireland, 'have good craic'!

Appendix

Apart from the named racecourses below, the copyright for the other photographs is held either by Healy Racing Photographers (HRP), which is based at Listowel, RoI, or by the Author (DSH) as follows:

Front cover - Punchestown Racecourse
Ballinrobe - HRP
Bellewstown - DSH
Clonmel - DSH
Cork - Cork Racecourse
The Curragh - DSH
Downpatrick - DSH
Down Royal - DSH
Dundalk - DSH
Fairyhouse - HRP
Galway - Galway Racecourse
Gowran Park - DSH
Kilbeggan - HRP
Killarney - Killarney Racecourse
Laytown - HRP
Leopardstown - HRP
Limerick - Limerick Racecourse
Listowel - HRP
Naas - DSH
Navan - DSH
Punchestown - DSH
Roscommon - Roscommon Racecourse
Sligo - HRP
Thurles - DSH
Tipperary - Tipperary Racecourse
Tralee - Tralee Racecourse
Tramore - Tramore Racecourse
Wexford - HRP
Epilogue - DSH
Back cover - DSH

Printed in Great Britain
by Amazon